TONGUE-IN-CHEEK STYLE FOOD-IN-MOUTH EXPERTISE

"The book is based on a simp' ﹍﹍﹍﹍﹍﹍ ' on
where to grab a tasty, affordab ﹍﹍﹍﹍﹍﹍
neighborhoods than people wh ﹍﹍﹍﹍﹍﹍ of
the work day? . . . You always a ﹍﹍﹍﹍﹍﹍
confirms it in enough detail that, ﹍﹍﹍﹍﹍﹍ you will be
more than tempted to take his di﹍
—Mark Brow﹍ ﹍﹍ago Sun-Times, May 25, 2004

"As soon as The Streets & San Man's Guide to Chicago Eats hit our desk, we went out and tried a couple of author Dennis Foley's picks. Boy were they good! Foley's choices are mostly no-nonsense places that emphasize hearty servings at great prices, often in neighborhoods the critics never hit."
—Chicago Sun-Times, Food, June 2, 2004

"What is significant about this book is that its author knows just about every Chicago-area hole-in-the-wall lunchroom named Chuck's, Vito's, Lalo's, Frank & Mary's, Sammy's, O'Donovan's and so on, clean neighborhood eateries where you can get a good burrito or sub at a decent price . . . A man who rides around all day in one of those big blue trucks is bound to know what he's talking about."
—Henry Kisor, Chicago Sun-Times, May 30, 2004

"These aren't eateries that show up in the typical restaurant guide. Foley leans toward meat and potatoes, and he likes to eat in taverns. The emphasis is on places you can get a hearty midday meal for just a few bucks. Also, unlike many guidebooks, this book spans the city, including Northwest Side and South Side neighborhoods that tourists rarely see."
—Leah Zeldes, Lerner newspapers, June 2, 2004

"[Foley's] reviews are peppered with wit, sarcasm and humor that only a city worker like the Streets and San Man can offer."
—The Villager, June 2004

THE STREETS AND SAN MAN'S GUIDE TO CHICAGO EATS

Dennis Foley

First Edition

LAKE CLAREMONT PRESS

4650 North Rockwell Street • Chicago, Illinois 60625
www.lakeclaremont.com

The Streets & San Man's Guide to Chicago Eats
Dennis Foley

Published May, 2004, by:

4650 North Rockwell Street
Chicago, Illinois 60625
773/583-7800
lcp@lakeclaremont.com
www.lakeclaremont.com

Publisher's Cataloging-in-Publication
(Provided by Quality Books, Inc.)

Foley, Dennis, 1960-
   The Streets and San man's guide to Chicago eats / by Dennis Foley. -- 1st ed.
   p. cm.
   Includes index.
   LCCN: 2003107615
   ISBN: 1-893121-27-5

   1. Restaurants--Illinois--Chicago Guidebooks.
2. Chicago (Ill.)--Guidebooks.   I. Title.

TX907.3.I32C435 2004   647.9577'311
                                QBI03-200968

Printed in the United States of America by United Graphics, based in Mattoon, Illinois.
08 07 06 05   10 9 8 7 6 5 4 3

Thanks to my bride, Sue, for putting up with all of my nonsense over the years; to my three sons, Matt, Pat, and Mike, who are the greatest gifts I have ever received; to Sam Weller at Columbia College for encouraging me to let the Streets and San Man talk; and to the lads in the City of Chicago's Department of Streets and Sanitation for convincing me to do away with brown bag lunches years ago.

Publisher's Credits

Cover design by Timothy Kocher. Interior design by Todd Petersen. Interior layout by Susan Petersen. Editing by Bruce Clorfene. Proofreading by Karen Formanski and Sharon Woodhouse. Index by Karen Formanski and Sharon Woodhouse.

Notice

TABLE OF CONTENTS

INTRODUCTION

So here's my scoop. I work for the City of Chicago—as an electrician to be exact. You might have seen me out on the road before, or at least one of my co-workers. We drive around the city all day in those dark blue and baby blue vans and trucks with the words City of Chicago, Department of Streets and Sanitation notched alongside the doors. If you haven't seen us on the road, perhaps you've seen one of us parked in an alley during break with a newspaper stuffed in front of our face. Streets and San workers like to read newspapers. It helps move the day along.

Now, sure, we get our work done every day, and we also stay up on current events with all the newspaper reading we do, but ask any Streets and San guy what he truly enjoys most; go ahead and ask him what he looks forward to every day, and the answer will be—lunch. That's right—lunch. Any reasonably intelligent Streets and San guy—and some

say those can be far and few between—will map out his day according to where he wants to eat lunch.

Now, let's make one very important thing clear from the get-go. I've been driving these city streets for many a year now, and as such, I know where some of the best food joints in the City of Chicago are. No, I'm not talking about those expensive, high-falootin' places. Not at all. Any clown with a paisley tie wrapped around his throat can show you those. When Streets and San workers head to lunch, we don't go to many white tablecloth joints. Sure, you'll find a few of those in here, but if that's what you're looking exclusively for, then your nose is in the wrong book. See, essentially, Streets and San guys are bargain hunters, and we're not real big on fighting off high cholesterol, either. In the following pages, you will find some of our favorite eating spots, places where you will not only get a good bite to eat at a good price, but places where you can also taste some of the culture that our neighborhoods have to offer at the very same time. Enjoy and eat big.

**A note about the structure and organization of the eateries in this book: there is none. I'm a firm believer in letting the potato chips fall where they may. If you're looking for a place to eat in a specific area of the City, check out the Location Guide in the Index (pp. 116–117).

Ratings

Every lunch spot in this book has received one of the following ratings:

🍴🍴🍴🍴 Excellent

🍴🍴🍴1/2 Very Good

🍴🍴🍴 Good

If a place puts out grub that falls below three forks, then you won't find it in this book. Being a true blue Streets and San man, I only recommend eateries that match my work habits. Get the picture?

Prices

Every meal in this book can be had for less than $10 (except for the few that are noted); most can be had for under $7.50; and some for under $5. That way you'll have plenty of leftover cash for your kids' college fund or to get your wife some new lingerie for your anniversary. Ah yes, there's almost nothing that can match the sight of a lovely lady waiting on a bed dressed in the lingerie you just bought for her, unless, of course, it's a lovely, hot meal or sandwich from one of the eateries in this here book.

GOOD GRUB— PART ONE

He who eats a good lunch always carries a big smile.
—Confucius's illegitimate stepson, Ralph

Bari Foods
1120 W. Grand Ave., Chicago
312/666-0730   **Rating:** 🍴🍴🍴

This deli is a throwback to the good old stores from the days of yore. Nice people, great chow, and good service are the norm in this establishment. If you want the ultimate Italian sub, Bari's is a must for you. For $4, one of the fellas who works the back counter will put together a sandwich that will make you fall to your knees and thank God for giving us humans the sense of taste. Mild giardiniera, hot giardiniera, no giardiniera—have it your way. The boys at Bari will be more than happy to comply. What you'll leave with will be a nine-inch sub on hard bread with all the good stuff (capicolla, Genova salami, mortadella, provolone, as well as lettuce, tomato, etc.) ready to be dropped down your throat. If you're up in the three-

hondo range (that's 300 pounds for the Streets-and-San-lingo-illiterates amongst you), you may want the 12-inch sub, which you can get for an extra buck. I usually get the nine-incher and bring half of it home for my bride. Later that night, in appreciation of my good deed, she'll usually get a little frisky with me when the lights go out—if you know what I mean. So not only does Bari's put out a great sub, but it can improve your love life too.

The Skinny on Bari Foods:

All in the Family, Part II

There's no Archie Bunker, no Edith, no Meathead, but if you stop by Bari Foods, you'll quickly find that this deli is all about family. Brothers Frank and Ralph Pedota have owned Bari since 1988. Prior to that time, Frank and Ralph learned their trade at the hand of their father who worked at the very same store for nearly 40 years.

"Frank actually started working here in 1964," Ralph said. "I came in a few years after that. We were just kids, 12 or 13, but we were glad to help out. My father brought us in on the weekends to pitch in."

After stints in the army for Ralph and college for Frank, the Pedota brothers returned to the store for keeps in the mid-1970's. Following the tradition set by their father, Frank and Ralph have both put their own kids to work in the deli.

"All of my kids have worked their way through this place," Ralph said. "My youngest is 23. They've all put their time in to help work their way through school." Pointing to his brother's son, Frank Junior, Ralph added, "And now young Frank is here helping, too." At 19, "he's the oldest kid in his family, and he's working here while he goes to UIC."

The sense of family goes far beyond bloodlines at Bari. Stop in during a busy lunch hour, and you'll find the back counter bustling with activity as the helpers weave their way around and toss insults at each other as they put together orders. The sight might remind you of a big family putting the finishing touches on their Thanksgiving meal before they actually sit down to eat. You're certain to find Miguel Carbajal, the self-proclaimed "second in charge," barking out commands to one of the other helpers and then giving a playful elbow to one of the other guys just for kicks.

Don't leave this place without that sub you came for, and as long as you're here, make sure to take some lunchmeat home. Bari puts together a fine array of top quality lunchmeats. "Frank only picks the best meats," Ralph said of his older brother. "Hands down, the best. That's what makes our subs so good." And while you're at it, snatch a jar of Ralph's homemade giardiniera from the shelf, too. The hot is guaranteed to put a hole in your belly. Believe me, I know. ∎

Lincoln Tavern
1858 W. Wabansia Ave., Chicago
773/342-7778   **Rating: \\\½**

The lunch crowd at the Lincoln Tavern in the heart of the Bucktown area is always entertaining. Run by a trio of Poles, this place serves up a regular menu of hot sandwiches as well as daily specials. I highly recommend the corned beef. This mountain of a sandwich ($6.50) is guaranteed to make your arteries howl. The steak sandwich is also a winner at $5.50. And hey, since this is a tavern, guess what? Not only can you get a great hot lunch, but you can swill a few cold beverages as well—not that the Streets and San Man ever does that, mind you, but you might want to.

If you catch young Stash, the bartender, on a good day, he might do something more than grunt at you. Also since

this is a family-owned joint, the fireworks will fly on occasion. Ah, yes, there's nothing quite like munching on a quality lunch while the proprietors bark insults at one another. Who needs a good lunch-time soap opera when you can get live entertainment like this?

Stop into one of the many shops along North Avenue for some fun. I highly recommend Quimby's at 1854 W. North Ave., a book and magazine store with a rather eclectic gathering of materials.

Vito and Nick's
8535 S. Pulaski Rd., Chicago
773/735-2050   **Rating: **

Pizza is the order of the day here. I must confess that I have never sampled anything else in all my visits to this place. Well, almost nothing. Sure, I've tried their salad before. It's crisp and fresh, but apparently they've never heard of cucumbers or green peppers or onions or celery. Iceberg lettuce and two cherry tomatoes is all you'll get if you make a play on the salad, but, hey, the locals don't come to V & N for the salad. This pizza ($11.50 for a large sausage) is one of the best and most unique on the South Side. You won't find Chicago-style deep-dish here. Rather, what you'll find is the ultimate in thin-crust pizza. It's paper thin and cut into bite-sized minnies that melt in your mouth.

Make sure you order some beverages while you wait for

your pizza, and expect to go through several. The wait-resses here were around when Abe Lincoln was President, and their arthritic legs don't move so fast. If you'd like, you can also kill some time by staring at the carpeted walls. That's right. The walls in this joint are carpeted. But when your pizza arrives, the wait and carpet-staring will be well worth it.

Hot Tip from Kev the Shoe:

It's All in the Sauce

Gunboats: that's what we call Kevin Leary's feet. A Streets and San telephone specialist, he's also the proud owner of a size 16EEE shoe, or some strange configuration like that. As such, he always has a difficult time getting a new pair of work boots. Streets and San lore tells of how the last pair of boots Kev the Shoe bought were sewn together by a horde of Alaskan Inuits and then airlifted in from Anchorage. Buying work boots may be a difficult task, but having big feet, according to Kev, can be a blessing as well.

"Sometimes, if I pack away too much food at lunch, I might get a little wobbly when I first get up from the table. But that's when my big feet come into play. If I'm feeling a bit tippy, my feet help balance me out. They keep me steady."

If you gave Kev an hour or so, he'd probably fill your ears up with how much he likes the pizza at his favorite place, Vito and Nick's.

"I used to put a whole large Vito and Nick's pizza away by myself when I was younger. But now I have to watch myself. It's harder to keep the weight off."

Vito and Nick's super thin pizza has been a favorite with South Siders for almost 50 years.

"That's what I like most," Kev says. "The thin crust. It really makes the pizza. In fact the crust is so thin that it can dry out sometimes. That's why I always order my pizza with extra sauce. It's a tad bit sloppy, but it keeps the crust moist." Kev doesn't hold back when he adds these final thoughts. "If you want a good Pizza, go to V & N. It's the best damn pizza in Chicago. Go for the extra sauce too. You won't be sorry." ■

Kincade's
950 W. Armitage Ave., Chicago
773/348-0010   Rating: \\\

It's very rare that you'll find a few Streets and San vans parked in front of any Lincoln Park eatery. We generally try to hide from all things yuppy and from places where it's tough to park an over-sized van. Kincade's, however, is one of the exceptions. We'll always find room to park the van—even if it means nudging a BMW a few inches forward and bumpering a Mercedes a few feet back. The specials in this joint make it worth the trip. Twenty-cent jumbo chicken wings are available on Tuesdays and Thursdays, and $1 half-pound burgers are ready to be inhaled on Mondays. With prices like these, you'll still have loads of money left in your pocket after lunch perhaps to bring a bouquet of roses home to your wife or your girlfriend, or, better yet, to both. So go ahead and order up 10 or 20 wings and have at it, or come to Kincade's with a group of 10 and order up 250 wings. We do it every now and again. We call it "The Bone Fest." The winner is the guy with the biggest pile of bones on his plate at the end of the meal, and of course, the winner doesn't pay. Call in advance, as the specials can change weekly or monthly.

Grand Central Station
5726 W. Grand Ave., Chicago
773/637-6376   Rating: \\\

Close to Area 5 Police Headquarters, this tavern serves up excellent pork chop sandwiches and burgers ($4.75 with fries). You'll feel right at home with the owner, bartender, and regular patrons. They're a friendly lot who will suck you right into their conversation as you nibble away on your chow. If you plan to be working in the area for a few days, let the owner know and you should make a few suggestions as to what you might like for lunch. He'll go out and get the grub for you and then cook it the way you like it. Now, that's what the Streets and San Man calls service.

M & J Lounge
2701 W. 35th St., Chicago
773/847-9151   Rating: \\\½

If you ever find yourself in the vicinity of Cook County Jail around lunch-time, just remember—M & J Lounge is a mere four blocks away. Who knows? Maybe you just spent the morning visiting your mother over at Cellblock 10 and you worked up a good appetite listening to her plans to break out of the clinker. Here's my advice: turn a deaf ear to your Mom and, instead, listen to those hunger pangs. The folks at M & J's will take care of you. This blue-collar establishment serves up a good selection of hot lunches for just over $5, the best of which are the beef stew, breaded pork chops, meat loaf, and roast pork. Since these lunches all come with healthy heapings of potatoes and veggies, tradesmen galore can be found here. So order up a meal and

DETOUR Take a walk or drive past the criminal courthouse that adjoins the county jail if you have the time. Many a fabulous trial has been held at 26th and Cal, as the locals call it. The architecture alone is phenomenal. When you look at this old courthouse with its grand columns and huge vanilla bricks staggered neatly atop each other, you might expect to see Julius Caesar himself come walking out beneath the columns ready to toss pennies to the peons waiting on his every word. Just when your eyes are about to trick you into thinking you're in ancient Rome, you'll hear the roar of a CTA bus spitting out clouds of black smoke into the air as it roars past, and that will bring you back to reality. Believe me; it will. If you'd prefer to people-watch, 26th and Cal is always a great place to give your peepers a workout. You'll see lawyer-types hustling to and from the courthouse, some of whom will have big, gold rings on their fingers and size-12 gym shoes on their feet. You might find others wearing bright orange or yellow suits that look like you could light a cigarette off them. Those are the defense attorneys. The state's attorneys will be dressed in conservative blue, black, or brown suits, with either wingtips, penny loafers, or pumps on their feet. You'll also see plenty of low-life gangbangers and other assorted punks strutting their way towards the courthouse steps—playing it cool, their baggy pants dragging along the sidewalk as they move. No two days are the same at 26th and Cal, so it's always worthy of a visit.

have a seat at the bar or at one of the many tables. There's plenty of room. The food will hit home for you.

Lawrence's Fisheries
2120 S. Canal St., Chicago
312/225-2113   Rating: \\\

Whatever sort of fish you want, you can get it at Lawrence's. The specials are numerous and reasonably priced. The shrimp dinner ($6.90) comes with a half-pound of tasty, good-sized crawlers, fries, bread, and an excellent sauce. Lawrence's is open 24 hours. You may like it so much you may choose to do the Lawrence's Fisheries Marathon, where you eat breakfast, lunch, and dinner at this ageless gem all in the same day. It's been done before; believe me, I know. Though there are plenty of seats available inside, I prefer to sit outside when the weather cooperates. The Chicago River flows behind, so grab a seat near the shore's edge and watch a powerboat or a kayak pass by. I usually taunt the boaters by waving a tasty fried shrimp at them. You may want to do the same. Sure, they've got nice boats, but you've got a half-pound of shrimp sitting in front of you. Believe me—you're better off. The shrimp here will melt in your mouth.

Grant's Grill and Gallery
11045 S. Kedzie Ave., Chicago
773/238-7200   Rating: \\\

This Mount Greenwood diner is an oldie and a goodie. Grant's has been dishing up "Wonderburgers," curly fries, and thick shakes to generations of locals for near half a century. Sure you can get a tasty reuben or a grilled chicken sandwich, but to get a true feel for this place, take the Streets and San Man's advice: throw your elbows up on the counter and order the double-cheeseburger basket, complete with an order of curlies. For $4.15, you'll know why this place has been a favorite with the Southside Irish since 1954.

Chuck's BBQ
5557 W. 79th St., Burbank
708/229-8700   **Rating: **

Okay, so this place isn't in the city. So what! When you get the craving for a Southern-style, pulled-pork sandwich, Chuck's place definitely fills the bill. Several places that serve pulled-pork sandwiches have sprung up in the Chicago area in recent years, and a few of them do a pretty darn good job, but if you want to experience an authentic Southern-style sandwich, Chuck's is the place to go. Pick your poison—hot or mild sauce, and go at it. For $5.50, you'll get a pork sandwich lathered with sauce and two sides (corn, fries, mac, beans, etc.). Personally, I always order a double-dose of beans whenever I go to Chuck's and then spend the remainder of the afternoon gassing my partner to death in the van. Yeeeeeeeh hah! Being a Streets and San guy is such fun. But hey, let's get back to Chuck's. Try a soup, if you feel so inclined. Chuck offers several good soups, as well as excellent gumbo and jambalaya. They're all worthy of a gander.

Laschet's Inn

2119 W. Irving Park Rd., Chicago
773/478-7915   **Rating:** 〰〰〰〰

You'll feel like you just walked into a tiny pub in the Bavarian Alps the moment you pass through the door. Beer stein after beer stein hang from the ceiling, and there are lots of neat photos and prints that scream *kraut* right at you. All lunches are $5.95 and you get a nice deal for that price. A cup of soup comes with every meal. Try the burger. You'll get a half-pound of tender cow cooked just right and with all the trimmings, too. The smoked pork loin is another of my favorites and comes with fries and kraut, as do all the lunches. My Aunt Myrtle is a German, and she's a heck of a cook, but this place even matches some of the grub she puts out. Laschet's opens at 2 p.m., so make plans for a late lunch if you find yourself heading here.

Frank and Mary's Tavern

2905 N. Elston Ave., Chicago
773/588-9628   **Rating:** 〰〰〰〰

Located within a few stone throws of the former site of Riverview, Chicago's grand old amusement park, this tavern welcomes you into its arms with an Old Style sign swinging with the wind over the doorway. A sweetheart of a gal, Mary is as big and friendly as the meals she serves. Her brother, Frank, helps man the post whenever he's not in the hospital recovering from his most recent heart attack. He eats his sister's food, too.

All kidding aside, when I think about "home cooking," I think about Frank and Mary's place. For $5.25, you can feast on your choice of various meat dishes (meat loaf, beef, roast pork) with a healthy load of mashed potatoes and veggies on the side, and there's not a bad meal in the place. For just over a buck, excellent soups are also available. On Thursdays, there's a definite treat for the Irish or Italian amongst you: corned beef, cabbage, and potatoes for those who like to wear boxer shorts with shamrocks on them, or meatballs, sausage, and mostaccioli for the paisans. If you decide to go Italian, I'll guarantee you this: you won't finish. Not only will Mary toss a few gigantic meatballs or sausages on your plate, but she also heaps the mostaccioli on you, and when I say heaps, I mean it. Be prepared to feel fat and happy after this meal.

The Skinny on Frank and Mary's Tavern:

Home Cooking 101

When Mary Bartemes grew tired of her downtown commute in the early '70s and joined forces with her brother, Frank Stark, it was Standard Oil's loss and our stomachs' gain.

"I couldn't stand the commute downtown every day," Mary said with a laugh. "I had a good job with Standard, but the El, the traffic—I just couldn't take it any more." Mary's ex-husband predicted that her partnership with Frank wouldn't last more than four months. "We've been at it now for 30 years," Mary said proudly. "I guess he was wrong."

Soon after joining Frank, Mary quickly added some of her own favorite recipes to the tavern's lunch menu. "We came over from Germany in 1956," Mary said. "Many of the meals I cook have come down the line from generation to generation in my family."

If you walk through the door of Frank and Mary's

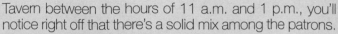

Tavern between the hours of 11 a.m. and 1 p.m., you'll notice right off that there's a solid mix among the patrons.

"We have CEOs from companies who come in, and they sit alongside the construction guys or city workers and everyone gets along," said Mary. "There's no preference. I treat everyone the same way here. I don't care if you have on a white shirt and tie, or if you have on a tee shirt. It's all the same."

So what is it exactly that brings this diverse cast of characters to their tavern? During the regular hours, some patrons might come to enjoy a few cold beers or a casual game of darts, but during that 11-to-1 time frame, all the patrons are here for the grub. Frank and Mary serve up good, solid, home-cooked meals, the sort that our mothers and grandmothers used to make.

As for me, I get a warm, fuzzy feeling in my belly whenever I dig my fork into any of the meals offered at Frank and Mary's. By the time I swallow that first hunk of meat, it's like I've climbed into the "way-back" machine and am feasting on a meal at my Irish grandmother's apartment. Grams was no fool. She knew how to take care of her grandkids. Believe me, she did. She knew that if she filled us up with enough meat and mashed potatoes and bread and veggies, chances were that we kids would fall asleep early in the evening. Probably right on the carpet in the front room. That way Grams could spend the night working the crossword puzzles she so loved, instead of breaking up the fights that often seemed to magically occur among the six of us.

Now take a look at Frank and Mary's menu. It might change slightly every now and again, but what won't change is the fact that it's good, basic home cooking.

Monday:	Pork Chops or Chicken (Cajun, BBQ, or lemon)	
Tuesday:	Schnitzel (pork or chicken) or Pot Roast	
Wednesday:	Meatloaf or Chicken Divan	

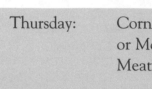

Thursday: Corned Beef and Cabbage
or Mostaccioli with
Meatballs or Sausage

Friday: Pork Roast or Fish (perch
or talapia)

All of these meals come with generous side dishes as well. The usual suspects are: mashed or boiled potatoes, macaroni, corn, peas, mixed veggies, potato salad, bean salad, and cole slaw, as well as bread and butter.

"The only thing I take out of a can are the vegetables," Mary said. "Everything else is home made. The food is real. And it's as close to home-cooking as you'll get."

Try it and find out for yourself. After you do, I'm certain you'll second Mary's opinion. ■

You're not far from Wrigley Field here. Every now and again, it's nice to work a half day, have a lunch at Frank and Mary's and then head over to Clark and Addison to watch the Cubbies play.

Sammy's Country Kitchen
5542 W. 55th St., Chicago
773/735-2802   **Rating:** ﹨﹨﹨

Picture this: your plane just landed at Midway and you're walking through the terminal getting ready to take a cab downtown. Being a man of wisdom, you gladly accepted the complimentary peanuts and pop offered during your flight, but it simply wasn't enough. It never is. Your stomach now craves food. Well, take my advice—walk right past all those

airport joints with their overpriced and low-quality chow.
Don't even bother to cast your eye on a vendor. Instead, hail
a cabby and tell him to take you to Sammy's. At Sammy's,
big—as in huge—is the name of the game. Big describes
everything on the menu. Daily specials as well as a regular
menu are always available. For $5, you can have a chopped
steak served with soup, potatoes, and veggies, and you won't
need an additional ounce of food for the remainder of the
day. Other excellent items are at the ready, and you should
walk out for under $8 for most things on the menu. You'll
see plenty of cops and airport personnel here, as well as some
guys from the 23rd Ward yard, just a biscuit flip down the
road. When you walk out of Sammy's, you'll have to loosen
your belt a notch. I guarantee it.

O'Donovan's Restaurant
2100 W. Irving Park Rd., Chicago
773/478-2100   Rating: \\\\\

In the heart of the St. Ben's community, the specials at
O'Donovan's make for a fine meal. At $8.95 for a full slab
and $6.95 for a half slab, you'll get some tasty fall-off-the-
bone ribs at a great price. The grilled-chicken sandwich is
tender and meaty, a regular melt-in-your-mouth meal.
There's also plenty of room for a big lunch group should you
need the space, and you can settle into a spot inside or grab
a table outside in the beer garden (heated as Chicago
weather demands). But take my advice. O'Donovan's is
known for it's burger-for-a-buck deal, where you get an
excellent hunk of meat cooked the way you want it and a
plateful of crispy fries for the cost of a couple of newspapers.

So go ahead and be a miser and order up two juicy burgers and flip the waitress a few bucks as a tip. You'll still walk out for around $5 and feel good about yourself.

Casino Restaurant
9706 S. Commercial Ave., Chicago
773/221-5189 Rating: \\\

This Croatian-owned establishment serves big sandwiches, and I do mean big sandwiches. Hot meatloaf, breaded veal, or beef come in a size that can easily feed two, and they're all priced at just over four bucks. This is the first joint I've ever been in that served a hot meatloaf sandwich—complete with gravy—on French bread with lettuce, tomato, and mayo. I know that might sound a bit strange, but trust me here. That condiment combo is actually quite tasty. There are also some good Croatian dishes should you choose to sample a more authentic fare. The soups are also excellent. As a matter of fact, I stop in on a regular basis for a soup to go. For two bucks and two bits, the Casino crew will load you up with a big soup, three to four hunks of Vienna bread, and enough butter to do a lube job on the family car. It's a meal in-and-of-itself.

Broken English is the language of the day at the Casino, and there are always a few interesting characters lurking about the restaurant tables ready to bend your ear with many an interesting tale.

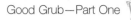

Taurus Flavors
8534 S. Stony Island Ave., Chicago
773/374-1872   **Rating:** \\\

This tiny fast-food joint serves up a good hoagie at a great price. $2.30 gets you a small hoagie, chips, and a pop on Wednesdays. There are specials on other days, too. Make sure you stand in front of the correct window when you place your order. There are two windows but neither is marked for pick-up or to order, but the regulars all know where to go, and if you happen to stray into the wrong line, they'll be certain to let you know about it.

Wikstrom's Gourmet Deli
5247 N. Clark St., Chicago
773/275-6100   **Rating:** \\\

Feel like listening to a few Swedes complain about high prices in America? Head over to this Andersonville favorite, and chances are you'll come across a few. This immaculate deli, filled to the gills with Scandinavian cheeses, candies, breads, and other goodies, offers up wholesome sandwiches for $3.50. Take your pick from the standard cold cuts like ham, turkey, and salami, or make a move for the pepper beef or meatloaf. The Swedes that run the place run a tight ship, so it'll run you an extra 50 cents for the lettuce and tomato. I'm a big fan of the meat-loaf sandwich myself. Go ahead and spring for the extra half a buck for the L & T and tell the counter lady to add some Swedish mustard, and put it on a Kaiser roll while she's at it. Toss in a pop and the assault on your pocket will come to roughly $5. The sandwich is fresh and tasty.

There are several tables up front near the picture window, so pull up a chair, enjoy the sights, and listen in on a few of those Scandinavian conversations like I told you to do.

 Andersonville is a great place to people-watch as its sidewalks and streets are filled with non-stop activity. From your post at a table in Wikstrom's, you can watch the action flow up and down Clark Street, or, if you prefer, you might want to join that flow and take a walk and stop in a store or two or three. Along the way, you'll find grocery stores, delis, restaurants, clothing boutiques, accessory shops, and more. Everything you want is here. Wikstrom's itself offers many great Swedish cheeses and accessories, and across the street at Erikson's Deli, you'll find another great place to browse for items that hail from the area that gave this neighborhood its name.

Hienie's Fish & Chicken
10359 S. Torrence Ave., Chicago
773/734-8400   **Rating:** \\\

East Siders. Have you ever heard of such an animal? Well I'm here to tell you that, yes, East Siders do exist, and they've been coming to Hienie's for shrimp and chicken for over 50 years. Nestled among the nearby coal mountains and abandoned steel mills, the folks inside this unpretentious shack kick out some quality grub. Grab a half-pound shrimp dinner ($7.75) or the three-piece chicken dinner ($3.33 on special days), go outside to your car, and sit on the hood to eat and to take a look around, if the weather permits. You can't help but get a feel for yesteryear in this area. As your nose takes in some coal fumes or the stench from one of the nearby, still-functioning mills, your mind may drift back to a time when this area was loaded with mill after mill, churning out steel products for use around the world. Most of the mills may have come and gone, but Hienie's is here to stay. As you eat that shrimp and chicken, you'll know why.

Top Notch
2116 W. 95th St., Chicago
773/445-7218   **Rating:** \\\

Although this place is known for its excellent Rhode Island-sized burgers, Top Notch offers far more than that. The milk shakes in this place are served the old-fashioned way, complete with a full glass and the extra in the stainless steel shake mixer. In case you didn't know it, the Streets and San Man loves milk shakes. My body does not function properly unless I sample at least three chocolate or cookies-and-cream shakes per week. Whenever I suck a cold, chocolate wonder from Top Notch down my throat, I usually try to balance it off a bit by ordering the always tasty, lo-cal tuna melt ($4.90 with fries). This sandwich is a guaranteed winner. Give it a whirl and let me know what you think. Top Notch is also a great place to bring your kids for lunch, if you feel like living dangerously. At this family-oriented establishment, the staff makes everyone feel at home.

Crabby Kim's
3655 N. Western Ave., Chicago
773/404-8156 Rating: \\\

Okay, okay, I admit it: we don't really come to Crabby Kim's for the food. Now don't get me wrong. The food in this joint is pretty darn good, and the specials are a bargain hunter's delight. The half-pound cheeseburger ($5.50, or $2.50 when it's the daily special) is a monster in and of itself, and the stuffed Italian sausage ($4.25) with a large heaping of peppers, mozzarella cheese, and Marinara sauce atop the sausage is also an excellent meal. In fact, everything on the menu is tasty, and they all come with a pickle and your choice of fries, potato salad, or a fruit cup. But we Streets and San men actually come to Crabby Kim's to see the bikini-clad waitresses. That's right—the staff here is dolled up in nothing more than skimpy bikinis. Crabby Kim's is a good place to go if your wife is pregnant, or if she hasn't exactly been interested in getting to know you lately. You can eat some top-notch grub, stare at scantily-dressed women and fantasize the afternoon away. Go ahead—call me a shallow man. I won't deny it.

Arch-View Restaurant & Lounge
3115 S. Archer Ave., Chicago
773/523-7550 Rating: \\\

If you ever get the inkling to eat a solidly-built sub or a ham on rye, and at the same time watch some old man sip his beverage of choice as he stares into another glass beside him holding his teeth, Arch-View is the place for you. This "old man's" tavern has a wide array of down-on-their-luck regulars who find their way to the bar counter most every day. They like to sip their beverages slowly to help move their day along, and every now and again, one of them will give his chompers a rest by dropping them into a glass of water. The cook draws a big lunch crowd by offering some outstanding hot specials (Salisbury steak, beef tips with noodles, and perch dinner—all for $6) and cold sandwiches. So, go ahead and grab a seat at one of the many tables and munch on a huge sub for $5, or, as I said, if you get that inkling—you can always find your way to the bar counter to do some teeth-in-the-glass watching while you chomp on your lunch.

Borinquen Restaurant
1720 N. California Ave., Chicago
773/227-6038   **Rating:** \\\\\

If you have never experienced Puerto Rican cuisine, then you need to flag a cab and head directly over to Borinquen. There are numerous authentic Puerto Rican dishes available here, but the most popular item on the menu—as well as my personal favorite—is the steak jíbaro (pronounced HEE-BAR-O). This steak sandwich comes smothered with cooked onions and is accented perfectly by a wonderful garlic sauce, as well as lettuce, tomato, and cheese. And then there's the best part—the fried plantains. This sandwich doesn't come served upon a standard bread. No way. Two fried plantains (cousins of the banana) form the bookends of this fabulous sandwich. You'll also receive a side of rice with your meal, and all this is yours for only $4.95. Though the price is right, don't even think about eating two of these babies. One will fill your belly for the remainder of the day.

La Scarola
721 W. Grand Ave., Chicago
312/243-1740   Rating: \\\\

This is one of the few white-table-cloth joints my part-
ners and I like to hit. Heavily adorned with Frank Sina-
tra and other Rat Pack photos, La Scarola offers a
fantastic lunch. What I like most is the oil and cheese and
bell pepper and bread and garlic they bring out for starters.
Ah yes, garlic. Ask for some fresh-cut garlic and your
waiter will bring a mound out for you. Go ahead and drop
a few tablespoons onto your plate and stick your nose in
it. It's a thing of beauty. There's nothing quite like that
lovely, stay-with-you-all-day-long odor of fresh-cut garlic.
Dump some of it in with your oil and cheese and sprinkle
some bell pepper in there, too. Rub your bread through it
and presto! That's good stuff.

I've never had a bad dish yet at La Scarola, but be prepared to splurge, at least by Streets and San Man terms.
You can get a few meals for under ten bucks (the $6.95
pasta primavera is good) but as long as you're here, you
might as well shake the coins out of your purse. We usually order a side of sausage and peppers, as well as a plate
of excellent calamari. At the meal's end, we'll walk away
for $15 a man. I love this place, but I feel compelled to
say that the food usually does some strange things to my
system, if you catch my drift. Maybe my poor, Irish body
can't handle all that oil and garlic and other good Italian
stuff. My dear Irish mother always told me that I should
just stick to potatoes.

My Boy Jack's
2547 W. 111th St., Chicago
773/238-0717

Rating: ♟♟♟½

This fast food diner picked up the vacancy left when long-time Beverly fast food king, Red's, was demolished to make way for the Beverly Arts Center. Some people might call that progress, but anytime a great eatery gets pancaked, I'd call it a damned shame. My Boy Jack's, just a few stone throws down the street from the former site of Red's, offers

My Boy Jack's is housed in the same building as Baseball Alley, a baseball training facility owned by Eric Pappas. Pappas, a former first-round draft pick (6th overall in 1984), played 13 years of professional baseball primarily with such organizations as the Cubs, Cardinals, and Angels. His best season was in 1993 where he was the everyday catcher for the Cards and maintained a stellar .276 batting average. So order up a chicken sandwich or whatever else tickles your fancy and grab a chair over in the baseball viewing area. Here you can eat your meal and watch a kid swat away at a few baseballs, or you might catch Eric or another instructor taking a kid through a hitting or pitching lesson. Feel free to ask the affable Pappas any questions you might have about the game he loves. He's always ready to talk shop. Ah yes, a little bit of baseball and a lot of good food. That's what I'd call a complete lunch.

quality fast food including three different chicken sandwiches ($3.95), all of which are pleasing to the eye and the belly. The standard grilled chicken sandwich offers up a hunk of marinated breast on a wheat bun and it's dressed to perfection with lettuce, tomato, mayo, mustard, and grilled onions. However, the Greek chicken sandwich is my favorite and is, as advertised, "A Must Try." Just picture that 6-ounce marinated breast grilled and cut into strips, and then spread out across a generous chunk of Italian bread. Top it off with onion, tomatoes, a cucumber dressing, and best of all, feta cheese, and you have one dynamite meal. If your mouth isn't watering after reading this description, then you might want to go see your medicine man to see if you still have a pulse. Trust the Streets and San Man here. This sandwich is delicious. You'll always find a few 19th Ward garbage trucks and Streets and San trucks parked outside of this joint. These guys know a good deal when they see one.

Dixie Kitchen & Bait Shop
5225 S. Harper Ave., Chicago
773/363-4943   Rating: \|\|\|

In the Hyde Park-University of Chicago area, Dixie Kitchen boasts a sampling of several Southern delicacies. For a change of pace, try the fried green tomatoes. This breaded appetizer might look a bit odd, but after you add salt and pepper and a splash of hot sauce, it really hits the spot. The corn bread johnnycakes are excellent. My recommendation: order the North Carolina BBQ. This tender shoulder sandwich is authentic North Carolina Que—meaning it's not smothered in sauce, but rather the flavor is smoked into the meat. Very tasty and comes with two sides of your choice for $7.95.

This is a rather lengthy driving detour but well worth the three-mile journey. Just east of the corner of 35th and Cottage Grove, where 35th dead-ends at the I.C. train tracks, you'll find the tomb of former U.S. Senator Stephen "the Little Giant" Douglas. His gravestone shoots up 40 feet into the sky, and a statue of the Little Giant himself stands proudly atop the marker. It's hard to miss once you're in the area. One of the great statesmen and orators in Illinois history, Douglas also has the distinction of defeating Abraham Lincoln for an Illinois Senate seat in 1858. The pair appeared together numerous times during that campaign to square off in the famous Lincoln-Douglas debates. Douglas later lost to Lincoln for the Presidency in 1860. The Douglas tomb stands upon grounds formerly owned by the Douglas family. Put this site on your don't-miss list, as you can't help but feel a strong sense of history while walking the meticulously maintained grounds and reading the various words of the statesman. The facility is staffed by knowledgeable workers, so feel free to ask questions.

Pompei
1531 W. Taylor St., Chicago
312/421-5179 **Rating:** \\\

For a different kind of pizza, I suggest Pompei. Order up a large (full tray) and what you'll get is a boxed, bakery-style pizza dripping with good taste. At $26, it's a bit expensive, but the Pompei folks claim it can feed up to 12 regular humans, or four to six Streets and San men. This "za" is well worth the extra coins, and when you share the expense with a few friends, you'll barely notice the five-spot leaving your pocket. I love the corner pieces. The edges roll up high and are extremely crisp. There was a time when I would knuckle it out with my comrades to see who would get these in-demand, corner pieces, but now that we're all getting older and somewhat wiser, we use "Rock, Paper, Scissors" to settle such disputes. Their new North Side location lacks the heritage of the original, but if it's your best option, give it a try: 2955 N. Sheffield Ave. (773/325-1900).

 **DETOUR** You can spend an entire afternoon bouncing about on Taylor Street from restaurant to restaurant. The area is always lively. For a change of pace, snag an Italian ice at Mario's, a tiny shack at 1068 W. Taylor (open for the summer season only, May–Oct.). Choose among the 20-some-odd flavors for your icy treat, or to avoid the long lines at Mario's, head around the corner to Carm's (1057 W. Polk) for a great ice without the wait.

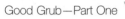

Lalo's
3515 W. 26th St., Chicago
773/522-0345   Rating: \\\\\\\\

When you're in the mood for Mexican, heed this advice: find your way to Lalo's and order anything you want. $5-$8 should cover the cost. Whether it's tacos, fajitas, quesadillas, burritos, or what have you—you'll like it—believe me. What I favor most about Lalo's, and what keeps me coming back time and time again, are all the pre-meal snacks. They throw a bowl of tasty soup at you the moment you walk through the door; then comes the never-ending stream of salsa and chips, as well as a container of some of the hottest jalapeños, carrots, and celery you can stand. After you and your mates down all of these scorching appetizers, don't be surprised to find golf-ball-sized beads of sweat tumbling down your head. To cool yourselves off, you'll need several glasses of water or Corona. With those in your system, you'll soon be back to normal and ready to take on your main course.

Other Lalo's locations:

- 2747 W. 63rd St.
  Chicago
  773/476-8207

- 4126 W. 26th St.
  Chicago
  773/762-1505

- 1960 N. Clyborn Ave.
  Chicago
  773/880-6581

- 500 N. LaSalle St.
  Chicago
  312/329-0030

Grizzly's Lodge
3830 N. Lincoln Ave., Chicago
773/281-5112   Rating: ♨♨♨½

Got the urge for a little elk steak? Perhaps you feel the need for some venison goulash or a buffalo burger. Grizzly's Lodge offers up many off-the-beaten-path meals as well as standard fare. When you walk in this joint, you'll feel like you're on a safari. Animal heads of all sizes and shapes stare down at you. Some heads are so close to you, you might feel as if they're about to claim their brother or cousin from your plate and run back to the woods to re-assemble the poor guy. A few of the rather exotic meals can be a bit costly (wild boar chops—$24.95, quail primavera—$16.95), but most can be had for under ten bucks, and there are always several hot-lunch specials for $4.99. The specials provide a bit of everything: soup or salad, a burger, or beef or chicken sandwich, fries or tater tots, and a drink. Take your time eating. You want to enjoy this place. As they advertise, you definitely get a North Woods feeling when you're here.

Izalco Restaurante
1511 W. Lawrence Ave., Chicago
773/769-1225   Rating: ♨♨♨

Affable owner David Velis once served an all-you-can-eat Salvadoran buffet for a measly $5.99. This was one of my favorite buffet stops in the city as there were over 30 items to choose from, including desserts. Talk about a joint where you could spend a few hours dropping mounds of great chow down your throat—this was definitely it. Well, the buffet may be gone, but the good food still remains at Izalco. For $5, there are plenty of good bargains, including my favorite, the ranchero steak, which, in addition to offering loads of great, spicy meat, comes with a healthy heaping of rice and refried beans—as do all the $5 specials. Ask for some *ejotes* (green beans with scrambled eggs) or the *pupusas de masa* (stuffed corn-meal tortillas with your choice of meat) if you feel like trying something in addition to the specials. Mr. Velis is also well-equipped to meet your cold-cut cravings should you find yourself in a sandwich mood. A 5-spot will take care of your sandwich, a drink, and your choice of a soup or French fries. Make sure to mark Izalco on your map when you're in the area.

O'Leary's Public House
541 N. Wells St., Chicago
312/661-1306   **Rating:** \\\

So maybe you just walked out of a Daley Center courtroom after finalizing your divorce, or perhaps you spent a frustrating morning waiting in a long line to pay a bill at City Hall. Whatever the scenario, you might need to blow off some steam, and I have just the place for you. Head north on Wells Street to O'Leary's. The three-block walk will do you good, and it won't put too much wear-and-tear on your loafers. You can check your problems at the door, and then order a burger, or you might want to go with the mostaccioli or chicken parmesan sandwich (both $6.95) if they're on the specials sheet. All these meals will be prepared to your liking and may just give you a new outlook on life. At O'Leary's the grub is good, the staff is friendly, and you're guaranteed to leave with a smile on your face.

No, this place won't make you forget those divorce papers in your pocket or the water-bill receipts in your wallet, but you will feel a little fatter and a lot happier.

Calabria Imports
1905 W. 103rd St., Chicago
773/396-5800   Rating: \\\

This long-time Blue Island favorite just recently relocated to Chicago's Beverly neighborhood. Good service and friendly smiles are the norm in this cozy deli. Daily hot sandwiches and pasta specials run $3.00-$6.00 and you won't find one that will make your taste buds throw up the white flag. The "Freddy," a skinless, flattened Italian sausage sandwich with mozzarella cheese, sweet peppers, and red sauce on French bread, is guaranteed to hit the spot. It comes with a heaping of fries and is priced right at $3.50. Make sure you bring some of the Italian Sausage home from this place. This meat makes one of the best backyard grill-cooks I've ever had.

Fontano's Subs
2151 W. 95th St., Chicago
773/881-7884   Rating: \\\½

With several locations available, it's a good feeling for the Streets and San Man to know that Fontano's Subs, like a good friend, is never too far away. In Fontanoland, they load all the goodies on their subs ($3–$4.25 for a 6-incher) and they're for the taking with names like: "The Blockbuster," "The Wiseguy," "The Big L—All Italian," and so on. The standard turkey, corned beef, and roast beef subs are also on the menu. I usually get the Italian. It's a good sandwich and though I usually only order the 6-incher, it's plenty. They load you up with meat, giardiniera, olives, pickles, lettuce, tomatoes, and it is one big, wonderful, sloppy mess, and when I say sloppy, I mean it. Make sure you have a spare pair of jeans available should you choose to eat this sandwich on the run in your car.

A few other Fontano locations:

- 1058 W. Polk St.
  Chicago
  312/421-4474

- 20 E. Jackson Blvd.
  Chicago
  312/663-3061

- 333 S. Franklin St.
  Chicago
  312/408-0555

Mom & Dad's Deli
6435 S. Central Ave., Chicago
773/767-DELI   **Rating:** \\\

Rooted amongst the factories that border the area due south of Midway Airport, Mom & Dad's Deli brings in the factory workers and locals in droves. Subs and sandwiches galore are available. You can't go wrong with any of the $5.00 daily specials (Monday—roast beef, Tuesday—turkey, Wednesday—corned beef, Thursday—chicken salad, and Friday—tuna salad), served up on your choice of any bread or roll, along with a pop and soup. Bring your earplugs because you'll be in the take-off and landing path of Midway. Can you say noise pollution?

DETOUR Take a side trip to 63rd and Pulaski to see the Big Chief, the 20-foot-tall cigar-store Indian who stands proudly atop the building on the northwest corner. You might find a few arrows sticking out of the chief's back, but I've yet to see him tumble to the turf. The big fella's a survivor, I'm telling you. That's all well and good, but the main reason for my suggested visit to the chief is this: As you drive or walk east along 63rd towards the corner of Pulaski (near Bud's Flower Shop) the chief will show you why every-one calls him "Big Chief." That's right—his dillywagger is hanging out of his pants—or so it appears. As you inch nearer, however, you'll realize it's an optical illusion. What you think you see is actually Big Chief's thumb. But at first glance, it does look like the real McCoy. Take a drive by and see for yourself. My kids always caw like big, black crows whenever we take a drive past Big Chief.

Nicky's
5801 S. Kedzie Ave., Chicago
773/436-6458   **Rating:** ♙♙♙½

This is the home of the original "Big Baby" Double Cheese-burger. Many have tried to duplicate this burger and may even use the same name, but Nicky's is still the Big Baby king of the hill. I first came to Nicky's in 1975 when it was a tiny diner with a dozen or so stools wrapped around the counter. In those days, every order was shouted back and forth. Now, in its remodeled and relocated site, Nicky's food is just as good, but there's very little shouting going on.

Computers now do the trick. There are numerous good choices on the menu—ribs, Grecian chicken, gyros, or chicken salad—to name a few. You won't go wrong and the price is right ($3-$6). Take my suggestion—please try the Big Baby combo and make sure you get grilled onions on it; they make the sandwich. With fries and pop for under $4, this is the meal that made Nicky's famous.

Miceli's Deli
2448 S. Oakley Ave., Chicago
773/847-6873   **Rating:** \\\\

When you come to Miceli's, chances are you'll have to wrestle for a table with a few assistant state's attorneys and a few cops from the Criminal Courts complex at nearby 26th and California. Loads of these guys spend their lunchtime at Miceli's. But that's not necessarily a bad thing. Who knows—maybe you've got a current case yourself over at 26th and Cal. You might want to spring for lunch for everyone seated in the deli. Subtle bribery has been known to work wonders. In any event, it can't hurt. When you turn up in court, one of the fellas you treated might reward your generosity.

Hot and cold daily specials run about $5 at Miceli's, and they all come with chips and a pop. For you salad lovers, I highly recommend the tuna-steak salad. It's light, seasoned just right, and sure to fill you up. On Fridays the linguine-and-clam-sauce is a steal at $4.50. This is also a great place for Lenten meals.

DETOUR

Little Italy is a wonderful place to take a short walk. Pop into the different restaurants for a beverage, or wrap your arms around an old light pole on Oakley and imagine what the streets used to be like in a long forgotten time. You'll definitely get the neighborhood feel here. Aside from Miceli's, several restaurants (Ignotz, La Fontanella, Bruna's, Bacchanalia, and Il Vicinato) are open for lunch, so give them a try. Sure, these full-scale restaurants are a bit pricier, but you'll find something on every menu for under $10, and they all serve top-gun grub. You'd be wise to come back to one for a full-fledged dinner in the evening. Or just walk slowly along Oakley and let the smells that drift out of these restaurants form a lovely combat zone, a sort of friendly fire that your nose will certainly find pleasing.

Sean's Rhino Bar
10330 S. Western Ave., Chicago
773/238-2060   Rating: ☃☃☃

With a name like "Sean's Rhino Bar," this joint starts out on the right foot from the get go. But it doesn't stop with the name. The lunches are always on target. Try the juicy half-pound Rhino burger ($5.25) or the steak sandwich on garlic bread ($7.25). They're both winners. The thin-crust pizza ($13 for a large sausage), a favorite of mine, is one of the better pub pizzas you'll find in the city. We're not talking frozen microwave or toaster-oven pizza here, folks. Nope. At the Rhino bar, they do things right. Give the pizza a try and you can thank me later. This is also a great place to set up camp and spend the day during the Southside St. Patrick's Day Parade. And if you don't happen to know what the Southside St. Patrick's Day Parade is, then all I can say is: There's little hope for you in this big world of ours.

Polk Street Pub
548 W. Polk St., Chicago
312/786-1142   Rating: \%\%\%

Next door to Scarlett's Gentleman's club, this friendly pub has several interesting options to choose from. You can pick the standard fare from the regular menu, but I suggest you just say, "Gimme the special," and take whatever they throw your way. All of the specials are gut-pleasers and will rid your pockets of roughly $6.50. My favorites are the bruschetta burger and the chicken parmesan entrée. The burger is made of a big heaping of sirloin dressed up with a tasty bruschetta mix and topped with mozzarella cheese. The chicken parm comes with a large hunk of chicken filet covered with Sicilian sauce and mozzarella over a large bed of angel-hair pasta. The two lasses that work the bar during lunch are always sassy and ready to throw barbs at any and all patrons. So come prepared to do battle. A lunch spent at Polk Street Pub is always a lively affair.

DETOUR

Two blocks south of the Polk Street Pub, you'll find the Chicago Fire Academy. Set on the very site where Mrs. O'Leary's cow allegedly kicked over the lantern that started the Great Chicago Fire, this is where the new recruits are trained to become firefighters and also where veterans return to further hone their skills. You might get lucky and drive past the Academy on a day when the recruits are busy hustling up and down ladders in the back parking lot, carrying huge chunks of gear on their backs. But you don't need to find the recruits in action to have a good visit; the lobby alone is a virtual mini-museum, housing several interesting artifacts from ancient firefighting devices to current hoses used in battle. You'll find an excellent pictorial and verbal history of the fire department offering information on some of Chicago's most well-known blazes. Finally, you can't help but be moved by the display featuring the badges of the firefighters who have lost their lives in the line of duty.

BREAK TIME

After I put in four good hours for the city, I always reward myself by going to one of the lunch establishments in this here book. I'll usually meet up with a comrade or two or three or more to discuss the happenings of the day so far and enjoy the break. As such, it's about time for us (writer and reader) to take a little breather. What do you say we shoot the breeze for a bit before getting on with the remainder of the reviews? Hey, you've made it halfway through this book, so go ahead and reward yourself. I have a couple of items I'd like to share with you during the break. So open your ears and prepare to be educated.

The Street's and San Man's Quiz

Test your knowledge of the contents of this book as well as your knowledge of the City of Chicago. The answers for several quiz questions can be found in the pages you've already read, some will be found in the pages yet to come, and some are matters of common knowledge. For answers, please turn to the following page.

1. How many Streets and San workers does it take to screw in a light bulb?

2. In the vicinity of what church was Al Capone's rival, Hymie Weiss, shot to death?

3. What does C.D.O.T. stand for?

4. If you want to see the ghost of the legendary Alderman Paddy Bauler, to what establishment should you go?

5. How does a City ghost payroller know he's had a successful career?

6. During the Cows on Parade exhibit, how many moo-moos were put on display?

7. Who claims to have invented the chili cheese dog?

8. If you plan to eat at Leif's, what should you make certain to bring with you?

9. What detour site can be found just off of 35th and Cottage Grove?

10. What size work boot does Kev "the Shoe" Leary wear?

Answers

1. Four. It takes one electrician to screw in the light bulb, one foreman to oversee the work, and two laborers to applaud once the job is actually completed. (source: common knowledge)

2. Holy Name Cathedral. (source: see page 51)

3. Most Chicagoans believe that C.D.O.T. stands for the Chicago Department of Transportation. However, those in-the-know fully understand that C.D.O.T. actually stands for the Chicago Department of Tony—in honor of the overwhelmingly huge number of Paisans employed by this department. (source: common knowledge)

4. Schaller's Pump. (source: see page 60)

5. At his retirement party, his co-workers keep staring at him and saying, "Who is that guy?" (source: common knowledge)

6. Approximately 320 cows. (source: The City of Chicago's Cultural Affairs office) Note: The Cultural Affairs office also estimates that the Cows on Parade brought in an additional $20 million in tourism revenues.

7. Fat Johnnie. (source: see page 75)

8. You need to make sure that you have, at minimum, a paper towel to pat down some of the grease from your meal. You might also want to use your shirt or a sock, if all else fails. (source: see page 68)

9. The tomb of Stephen "the Little Giant" Douglas. (source: see page 29)

10. Size 16EEE. (source: see page 9)

Grade Yourself (*See where you rate in the brains department*)

9–10 correct answers. Way to go, sunshine. You've shown off your brilliance. Your future looks bright. I see a job for you as a corporate raider, a meteorologist, or a writer of strange guide books.

7–8 correct answers. Not bad, buddy boy. You've done a fine job, but you aren't exactly the top dog in this group. With your faults, you might have to go on and become a criminal defense attorney, or even worse, a medicine man (a.k.a. a doctor). You have my sympathies, by the way.

5–6 correct answers. Congratulations. You are a middle-of-the-road kind of guy. You're just what the Streets and San Man is looking for. I'll be in contact with you soon to discuss some city job opportunities.

0–4 correct answers. Sorry. That's all I can say. If I said anything else, you wouldn't understand it anyway, you big dummy.

THE STREETS AND SAN MAN'S BLTCE&G RECIPE

After using up a lot of brain power on that quiz, I'll bet you're feeling a bit hungry. As a matter of fact, it wouldn't surprise me to learn you're completely famished. Tortuous exams always seem to have a way of draining one's energy. Before we get back to the reviews, I'd like to share a recipe with you, and after you study its finer points, feel free to pull out the pots and pans and have at it. It's just the snack you may need to get your exhausted self back on track.

Allow roughly 5–10 minutes to prepare this BLTEC&G (Bacon, Lettuce, Tomato, Egg, Cheese, and Giardiniera) sandwich.

1. In a large pan, fry up seven strips of bacon until they're good and crisp. Leave the grease in the pan.

2. Toss two slices of bread in the toaster.

3. Fry one large egg right in the middle of the bacon grease. While the egg is cooking, reward yourself by eating one or two strips of the bacon you just cooked. Make certain, however, that you eat no more than two pieces, as you'll want at least five for your sandwich.

4. Place the cooked egg on one of those beautifully bronzed pieces of toast and cover it with a slice of cheese. Place the bacon strips atop the cheese. This strategic placement of all items will ensure that the cheese gets nice and melted. Add lettuce and tomato to your liking and liberally douse the

whole mound with giardiniera (mild, hot, or super-hot) of your choosing. Complete the concoction by spreading a not-so-thin layer of mayo across the remaining piece of toast, and place said toast on top of everything.

What you'll have is not only a tasty sandwich that resembles a two-flat, but, more important, you'll have a snack that's certain to restore your depleted energy level. So now you know my secret: Not only can the Streets and San Man eat, but he's one whale of a chef as well.

GOOD GRUB— PART TWO

*Some seek happiness through love or money,
while the wise seek happiness in food.*
—Confucius's other illegitimate stepson, Franky

Club 81-Too
13157 S. Avenue M, Chicago
773/646-4292   **Rating:** \\\½

Parked along the alphabet avenues in the lovely neighborhood of Hegewisch, or "Head Squish," as some call it, Club 81-Too throws some good grub at you. The fried chicken dinner ($5.25) never fails to be a good buy, and the beef sandwich ($2.25) is made the same way today (on rye bread with grilled onions) as it was made when Papa Dombrowski first served it over 50 years ago. The Friday fish fry is a definite gamer. For $9, you'll get plenty of bite-sized perch filets, a heaping of fries, slaw, and some tasty radishes and green onions that will leave your breath smelling like a prince for the remainder of the day.

George Dombrowski and his brother Frank run the place, and they will welcome you with a wry smile, sharp

DETOUR ➡

Take a walk behind Club 81-Too and you'll run right into Wolf Lake, a Lake Michigan feeder. The locals say there's been so much crap dumped into this lake from the nearby mills, that catching sight of a three-eyed fish or a neon fish is a common occurrence. I just hope this isn't where George shops for his fish fry fixings.

wit, and many a story. After you've stared at George's surgically repaired elbow and watched him gimp around a bit on his bad leg, ask him about it. He'll gladly tell you about his days in Viet Nam. But once he gets going, plan on being there a while. The next time George tells a short story will be the first time he tells a short story.

The Skinny on Club 81-Too:

Staying Power

If you sat on a stool in Club 81-Too at lunch, you'd hear the usual corner-bar talk. In between bites of fried chicken, beef sandwiches, perch, burgers, or walleye, the patrons' chatter might hit the Bears, corrupt politicians, the new addition going up at so-and-so's place, and the casinos in nearby Hammond. Opinions fly at Club 81-Too as often as a salesman with frequent-flier miles. Whenever a change in topics occurs, you can rest assured that George is the one controlling the shift.

"Everybody in this place is entitled to their opinion," George said with a laugh, "but my opinion is the only one that counts."

A Viet Nam vet who has seen many things in his life, George doesn't believe in holding back.

"I love listening to what people have to say. I grew up in my father's bar, so I've been listening in on bar talk all my life. But I'm not here just to listen. Hell, no. I'll put my two cents in whenever I feel the need."

Club 81-Too has been in the Dombrowski family since 1945 when George's father opened it at 81st Street and Exchange Avenue. In 1981, a few years after Papa Dombrowski died, George and several family members moved the tavern to its current location, and here they have continued the family tradition of offering good food, good drink, and lively conversation.

"My brother, Frank, handles the restaurant end of things," George said. "I take care of the bar end for the most part. The fish fry is by far one of our biggest sellers. We give people a fair shake on the prices, and our food is good, so we have a lot of steady patrons. Sure, we get the neighborhood guys, but we also get the guys who are working in the area and hear about us. Word of mouth is our best advertisement."

In 1968, while serving in Nam, George suffered several severe injuries. The medicine men had to practically stitch parts of him back together. "I was only in Nam for two months," George said, "and then I got shot up. I spent the next two years in the hospital." To this day, George wears a heavy steel brace to support his leg. His surgically repaired arm slows him down a bit, but it hasn't stopped him.

"I'm still the fastest bartender on the South Side," he said with a chuckle. "Just you watch me." George walks out from behind the bar and ambles slowly toward the kitchen area with a food order in hand. His bad leg and arm slow his pace to a mere crawl. No, George isn't fast. Rather, he's a teller of tall tales and a man of dry humor. And much like the bar he owns, George has staying power; I'll take staying power over speed any old day. Just ask the turtle and the hare. ∎

Emerald Isle Bar & Grill
2535 W. Peterson Ave., Chicago
773/561-6674   Rating: \\\

This place smells just how a tavern should smell. Some establishments work so hard to get rid of that beer-soaked smell from the floor. At others, that smell just blends in until it becomes part of the surroundings, like a buddy you like to elbow up to the bar with to have a few. At the Isle, that smell blends in and becomes a welcome part of the surroundings. You can chow down on some quality grub and let the scent fill your nose. Irish brogues bounce off the walls, so come prepared to hear many with the Celtic gift of gab espouse their views. The chicken breast sandwich ($5.75) and the steak sandwich ($6.50) are just a few of the excellent items. There's always a daily special where you can get tacos, burgers, or beef sandwiches for a buck or two, and the Friday fish fry ($5.75) is a definite contender.

Mister J's
822 N. State St., Chicago
312/943-4679   Rating: \\\\

For you hamburger aficionados amongst you, Mister J's will take good care of your cow cravings. Jump in line with the cabbies, construction crews, and students from neighboring Loyola University School of Law to sample the wares. Try the Number 1 with cheese; that's my favorite. For under $4, you'll get a great burger with a wide choice of condiments (ketchup, mustard, mayo, onion, relish, kraut, lettuce, tomato, and more), french fries, and a shake or drink. For those with bigger appetites, give the

Dagwood a shot. It's a half-pounder certain to fill your belly for the remainder of the day. Everything on the menu is excellent and reasonably priced.

Walk over to Holy Name Cathedral just down the block at 725 N. State St. This beautiful church is worthy of careful study. It's also the site where several Chicago mobsters were sent to their graves. In the late 1920s, Hymie Weiss, a North Side mob boss and an enemy of Al Capone's, met his maker in front of the church. The spray of bullets from the tommy gun his killers used splattered many of the exterior's bricks and cut a religious sign attached to the church in half. In a similar '20s shooting, another Capone enemy, mobster Dion "Deanie" O'Bannion, was also shot and killed in front of Holy Name. That Capone—he sure had a strange way of relating to people, didn't he? And be sure to check out the Rush Street restaurants and shops, as well as Water Tower Place, a few blocks east.

Bertucci's
300 W. 24th St., Chicago
312/225-2848   Rating: \\\

This eatery kicks out a helluva chicken parmesan and breaded steak parmesan for only $6.75. Both come smothered in red sauce and veggies and a large bed of pasta. It's all there for you. And be certain to start the meal off with plenty of olive oil and bread and grated cheese. Don't hold back because they'll bring out loaf after loaf for you.

I like to take my wife to Bertucci's every now and again. The portions are large and she can never finish hers. It's all part of my plan. That means yours truly not only gets to eat my own meal, but I get to eat about half of hers as well. And you thought I wasn't smart. Shame on you. After you're ready to burst, walk it off and catch the sights in nearby Chinatown.

Swanson's Deli
2414 W. 103rd St., Chicago
773/239-1197 **Rating:** \\\

Numerous hot and cold sandwiches await you at Swanson's, where you'll always find several daily specials chalked on

Take a drive two miles north of Murray's (p. 53) and check out North Park Village at 5800 N. Pulaski. The former site of the Chicago Municipal Tuberculosis Sanitarium, it now houses a senior-citizens complex, Peterson Park, the nature center, and a smattering of city offices and departments. Inside the administration building, you'll find a room with photos of the place when it was a full-blown TB sanatarium, and over in the nature center, there's a trail that provides great viewing of birds and other critters. The nature center itself is a fun place to bring the kids as there are loads of hands-on artifacts, taxidermied animals, and family-oriented programs—such as star gazing and tapping maple syrup from trees.

the menu board—all solid buys. Grab a chili or a soup and a sandwich. I suggest the chicken salad on French bread with all the trimmings. For $4.75, you'll get a great sandwich, a pickle, and a side of slaw or potato salad. You may also want to bring home a pound or two of the chicken salad for the family to enjoy as it's one of the best salads in the city. I always score big points whenever I bring home some of this stuff. In fact, I always bring my wife a two-pound bucket of Swanson's chicken salad on Valentine's Day and on our anniversary. Ah yes, even the Streets and San man knows how to score big on the romance scale.

Murray's Pub & Grill
4553 N. Pulaski Rd., Chicago
773/478-6096   **Rating:** \\\½

Painted green on the outside and adorned with white shamrocks, this tavern lets you know that there will be plenty of touches from Ireland inside. The owners usually have an eye-catching lass or two from the auld sod working the kitchen and the nice thing is, the kitchen is right there in plain view. Watch as the girls scoop a nice bowl of tasty soup for you ($1.50, or comes with the meal), or cook up a nice pork-chop-and-potatoes meal ($5) or any other of the daily specials. Go ahead, have a pint as long as you're here. The Guinness is tasty and the Harp is cold, or so I've been told. This place has all the essentials: nice hunks of meat, potatoes, and cold beverages. So ask yourself, do you really need anything more than that?

Taco Joe
3458 W. 111th St., Chicago
773/429-0515 **Rating:** \\\

Taco joints are a dime a dozen, but this place kicks out some good chow at an excellent price. If you're in the Mt. Greenwood area, head over to Joe's and order a couple of steak tacos and a big bag of chips with salsa. You won't have to steal any money from your kid's piggy bank to cover the cost, either. Toss a pop into the mix and you'll walk away for about $5. You'll also find daily specials featuring fajitas, burritos, and tacos—all come with beans, rice, and a drink for the same low price.

Fogo de Chao
661 N. LaSalle St., Chicago
312/932-9330 **Rating:** \\\\

When it's a co-workers birthday, or if one of my work buddies just dumped the wife he's hated for 15 years, it's time to pull the big money from out of our socks and splurge. For $25, you can take a seat in this Brazilian eatery and munch until you drop. The wait staff will stand by at your beck and call. Feel like two or three filet mignons? Maybe you'd like some pork or chicken before you take on those two steaks. Thirteen different meats are waiting to be checked out by your taste buds at Fogo de Chao. The gauchos slice the meat from spits right in front of you, and you also get your fill of spuds, veggies, salad, fried polenta, and the house specialty—cheese bread; just flip your chip and the trusty gaucho will be there for you with more food. Outstanding is the key word here.

Tony's Beef
7007 S. Pulaski Rd., Chicago
773/284-6787   **Rating:** \\\½

Folks in the West Lawn and Marquette Park neighbor-hoods have been gobbling up the grub at Tony's for years. At about 11 a.m. on any day, the Streets and San vans and trucks start jockeying for parking position in front. Within minutes, the People's Gas and Com Ed guys usu-ally join in the fight for those prime spots. If it's an Ital-ian beef, a combo ($4.25), or a Poor Boy ($3.75) you want, the guys at Tony's will take care of you. Make sure to get an order of fries, too. Not only does Tony put out one of the best beefs/combos in the city, but the fries, sprinkled to perfection with a spicy seasoning, are also fab-ulous. If you decide on the Poor Boy, call ahead. It takes 10 minutes to make, but it's well worth the wait. The chili is also a great, quick fix.

Hot Tip from Pete the Russian:

Bring on the Combo

We all have days where we wake up, and the first thought that pops into our mind is: I need a combo. Ah yes, a combo—that luscious union of Italian beef and Italian sausage stuffed onto a roll dripping with gravy. If you haven't as yet awak-ened to such an image, then you might consider visiting your local head-thumper. With all those degrees, maybe he can help straighten your noggin out for you.

Whether you go dry or dipped or dripping with red sauce and cheese, there's nothing quite like a combo. Pete Pup a.k.a. Pete the Russian, the self-proclaimed King of the Combo, has been known to put away five or six combos in a week.

"In my opinion," Pete said, "you go ahead and eat whatever the hell you want, but if I was havin' my last meal—it'd definitely be a combo."

Pete's an electrician with the Streets and San Department, and his rather robust belly tells the story of his eating propensities. Like any good Russian, Pete comes to work every now and again looking like he slept in a vat of vodka. But hey, enough of Pete's drinking habits. Let's get back to his favorite meal, the combo.

"Beef is beef," said the King of the Combos. "You gotta know how to make the gravy in order to make a good combo. I like mine with hot giardiniera and sweet peppers, and I like it wet, too, but not soggy wet."

Pete could spend an afternoon talking over the best beef joints and combo huts in and around the city. When pressed to pick a few, he honed in on Johnnie's in Elmwood Park and Boston's at Grand and Chicago.

"Both of them places make a good combo," Pete said, "but Boston's is a little bigger. I ate two of their combos at one sitting once, but I didn't have no fries or nothing else with it that day." It's good to see that Pete laid off of the fries. Every Streets and San man has that health-conscious side to him.

"You got a couple of yahoos at Boston's," Pete said. "You got the Baldy Jack. He weighs about 350 pounds. He's the manager, and he's a nice guy, too."

Both Boston's and Johnnie's, according to Pete, serve excellent sausage with the combo. "Only problem is," Pete added, "you might get some 13-year-old cooking the sausage at Boston's every now and again, and he'll burn the shit out of it." Pete didn't want to leave the South Siders out, either. "And if you happen to be on the South Side, try Tony's at 70th and Pulaski. They put out a good combo there, too." ■

The Streets and San Man's Top Beef Joints:

Al's	1079 W. Taylor St. Chicago 312/226-4017
Boston's	2934 W. Chicago Ave. Chicago 773/486-9536
Jay's	4418 N. Narragansett St. Harwood Heights 708/867-6733
Johnnie's	7500 W. North Ave. Elmwood Park 708/452-6000
Pete's	7843 S. Stony Island Ave. Chicago 773/375-6001
Pop's	10337 S. Kedzie Ave. Chicago 773/239-1243
Roma's	6161 N. Milwaukee Ave. Chicago 773/775-2078
Tony's	7007 S. Pulaski Rd. Chicago 773/284-6787
Tore's	2804 N. Western Ave. Chicago 773/227-7595

Beggar's Pizza
3277 W. 115th St., Merrionette Park
708/385-3434   **Rating:** \\\\

I'm not big on throwing chains at you (Beggar's does have six stores), but the fact is, this joint puts out a fabulous meatball sandwich at a mere $4.25. Now, I don't know about you, but I don't like it when I order a meatball sandwich, and as I eat it, the meatball starts to crumble into a pile of ground beef. If I wanted a crumby sandwich like that, I'd just ask my wife to make it for me. The meatball served at Beggar's will stay firm and forgiving even after you beat it up a bit with your chompers. In fact if you pulled one of these little buggers out from the toasted bread, sweet peppers, mozzarella, and red sauce, I'd bet you could probably dribble it all the way home. It has that much bounce to it. Give it a shot. You won't regret it.

A couple of other Beggar's locations:

- 10240 S. Central
  Oak Lawn
  708/499-0505

- 3524 Ridge Rd.
  Lansing
  708/418-3500

DETOUR →

Truth is, when it comes to Beggar's, you're in the sleepy little town of Merrionette Park. There's not a whole heckuva lot to do here, but please heed this advice: Be careful when you drive along Kedzie, or along 115th. The M.P. police are very eager to deliver traffic citations.

D.A.'s Deli
2926 W. Columbus Ave., Chicago
773/778-4594 Rating: \\\\\

When you find yourself out south in the vicinity of 74th and Western, take a turn onto that angle street (Columbus) and make a stop at D.A.'s. Don't let the bulletproof glass at the order counter scare you off. The folks who run this joint are friendly and fast, and better yet, they serve whole-pound corned beef sandwiches for $6. That's right—one whole pound. Go ahead, try to imagine that full pound of corned beef sitting between two slices of rye bread, covered with a delicate smothering of mustard. Ah, yes, that's good eating. I'm foaming at the mouth just thinking about it. The steak hoagie (Sloppy Joe-Style) with mild peppers is also a solid choice for $5. Both sandwiches come with chips or fries.

Muskie's
2878 N. Lincoln Ave., Chicago
773/883-1633 Rating: \\\\\

Muskie's has been in business for over 50 years primarily because they offer up great burgers. Sure, you can get a tasty dog, chicken sandwich, or other fare, but this place is known for their cooked cow. So—when in Rome, do as the Romans do—order a burger and have them toss on whatever you like from the wide array of condiments. Tear into that burger ($3) and savor its tasty, charcoal-smoked flavor. With its steamed bun and juicy, made-to-order sirloin service, this is one of the best fast-food burgers in the city. When you finish, you'll know why Muskie's has been around as long as it has.

DETOUR When your meal is over, I suggest you take a nice stroll south on Lincoln. Powell's bookstore, a used-book emporium, is a half block up the street. Stop in here and wander about this warehouse.

You'll find plenty of bargains. Powell's is a book-lover's dream. Not in the mood for a book? Fine. Cross the street and head south another 50 yards or so to see the psychic. Ask her about your future. I've done it before. Who knows? Maybe she'll tell you you'll be lucky enough to land a Streets and San gig somewhere in the near future.

Schaller's Pump
3714 S. Halsted St., Chicago
773/376-6332   **Rating:** \|\|\|

In the heart of Bridgeport, this pub has been around since 1881 and has a long history of politics. Current and past aldermen, mayors, and other political types have frequented this pub over the years, and you can't help but get the feeling that many a deal has been cut here. Set directly across the street from the 11th Ward Regular Democratic Organization, chances are if you're sampling a daily special ($6-$7 for burgers, prime rib, and other meat-and-potato-meals), you might run into the ghost of the late, great Mayor Richard J. Daley, or you might even run into the ghost of legendary Alderman Paddy Bauler. Bauler ran the show in the 43rd Ward in his day but stories say his ghost likes to come south every now and again, and when he does, he makes Schaller's his stopping spot.

If you do run into Bauler's ghost, or the ghost of any other ward boss, you'll know right away. You'll feel their hands in your pants grabbing at quarters and dollars. Bauler's ghost is like every other alderman and ward committeeman. They always find a way to reach into your pocket.

DETOUR

As long as you've made your way to Schaller's to chase down some good grub as well as the ghosts of the past, you should drive by the home where the late Mayor Daley and the current mayor lived for many years. Until the current mayor's mother, Sis Daley, a great lady, recently died, she occupied this modest home at 3536 S. Lowe. Please be respectful. In the past, there was always an unmarked squad car parked in front of the house, but that detail ended when Sis passed away. This home is a piece of Chicago's history as this is where modern day Chicago politics was born.

Mi Esperanza
4757 N. Western Ave., Chicago
No Phone   **Rating:** 𝄃𝄃𝄃

Push through the door to this tiny dive, pull up a chair at the counter, and order up some tacos or any other Mexican dish. They're all good and priced right. Tacos run $1.50 apiece, and the hot sauce makes the taco. If you get a smile out of the señorita who works the counter, call me and let me know. I'll drive right over and snap a photograph of this momentous occasion. In all the times I've parked my arse at the counter, I have yet to see her flash her pearly whites. As long as you're here, stare at the boob tube with the rest of the yokels, but don't expect to find Oprah staring back at you from the screen. The tube is always glued to the Spanish stations. This is a great place to stop for a tangy bite, especially if you feel like trying out those few words of Spanish you know by heart. Muy bien.

La Milanese
3158 S. May St., Chicago
773/254-9543   Rating: \\\

For one of the best breaded steak sandwiches in the city, you better make sure you put La Milanese on your lunch list. The counter guys'll dip that steak in red sauce and then fold it into a healthy hunk of French bread. Sweet and hot peppers are there for the taking. It's not rubbery and chewy as are some of the steaks offered at other eateries, and it's yours for $6. Also worthy of a try is the La Milanese cheeseburger. This mean daddy ($4) comes with the proverbial kitchen sink. (Can you say mama-mia?) You'll walk out after eating the burger with so many different flavors in your mouth, your taste buds will be doing a tango for a week.

The Brick and Beam Pub
4630 W. Lawrence Ave., Chicago
773/777-4746   Rating: \\\½

Ask any city worker over at the 39th Ward yard (4605 W. Lawrence) where you can find a good chili shack, and they won't have to give you directions. Nah. They can simply raise a bony finger and point directly across the street to The Brick, a cozy pub with excellent food. For starters, order a large bowl of chili. It comes in a big, stainless steel bowl, and for about $3, it's a meal in itself. It has all the standard ingredients swimming around in it, with assorted secret spices. But the good food doesn't stop with the chili. Hell, no. The burgers ($4.50) and chicken sandwiches ($5) are great, and the ribeye ($6) is a definite steal. If you happen to be a South Sider, don't mention it to the other patrons. They have more jokes and remarks about South Siders than a leopard has spots.

The Skinny on The Brick and Beam Pub:

A Hole in One

Jim Hinds, the owner of The Brick and Beam Pub, has several passions in life, and among them are cooking and golf. While Jim's a respectable 19 handicap on the golf course, a princely score for an amateur, he's a definite pro in the kitchen.

"I've always cooked," Jim said. "I cook here at work. I cook at home. Even when my wife was alive, I was the one who always did the cooking."

When Jim first took over The Brick in 1978, there were only two items on the pub menu: burgers and hotdogs. As he remodeled the tavern, he expanded the grill area and added a steam table.

"I bought the steam table off a guy for $50," he said. "It's probably 50 years old by now, but the thing still works great."

The Brick now offers food from 11 a.m. until one hour before closing. Patrons can still order a burger or a dog, but they'd be wise to try one of the others items on the expanded menu. "Now you can get just about anything," Jim added. "We serve filet mignon, chicken gyros, reuben, and stuffed green peppers, to name a few. You name it and we got it."

And let me say this about the food at The Brick—it's all good. Jim has the Midas touch when it comes to the grill. Whether it's cooking up one of the standard menu items (ribeye, ground round, grilled chicken), or one of the daily specials, Jim always dishes up food that will meet with your taste buds' approval. If you find the stuffed green peppers ($5.25) on the Daily Special board, go for it. This mixture of meat, onions, corn, and tomatoes stuffed into two green peppers and served on a bed of rice is excellent.

Whenever I eat at The Brick, I get the notion that I'd like to sneak up on Jim at closing time, blindfold him and then whisk him away to serve the remainder of his life as my indentured servant. Of course, in my demented plan, Jim would never be allowed to leave the kitchen, and I would spend all my remaining days wolfing down the quality chow that Jim produces. Most guys fantasize about beautiful women. I, on the other hand, fantasize about food and kidnapping cooks. Go ahead, call me strange. I can't deny it.

When you come to The Brick, you'll feel right at home from the get-go. "We get some regulars from the neighborhood," Jim said, "but we also get people from all over. We get blue-collar guys, guys in suits, retirees, people with kids."

Stop by The Brick and say hello to Jim. Sure, he might shank a putt every now and again on the 18th hole, but in the kitchen at The Brick, he always puts the ball in the cup. ■

D'Amato's Bakery
1332 W. Grand Ave., Chicago
312/733-6219   **Rating:** \|\|\|

D'Amato's has several bakeries and eateries along the

Grand Avenue corridor. This one is a few blocks west of Bari Foods. If you're in the mood for a good Italian sub, but don't think you can drop the big Bari sandwich down your throat, then give this joint a try. For about $5, they'll dish you up a good sandwich with all the fixin's and a drink. If you feel like a piece of bakery pizza, $2 will get you a slice, and it definitely hits the spot. If it's your turn to cook the weekly pasta dinner for the little lady and your kids, you can snag several loaves of bread right here to accent what I'm certain will turn out to be a fabulous meal. D'Amato's is well-equipped to take care of all your needs.

Riverside Marina
13601 S. Calhoun Ave., Chicago
773/646-9867   **Rating:** \\\

Don't be surprised if you get lost trying to find this place. You won't be the first one. Take Torrence (2800 east) to the stop light at 136th Street, then a right. Follow the signs to the marina. You're at the far southern end of the

After you eat, walk down to the Calumet Canal. The locks that lead out to Lake Michigan are just 100 yards away, and the area bustles with activity in the summer. It's also fun to venture up and down the lines of boats in disrepair and pick out which ones once were winners, or the boats that could be winners should you decide to put the time and cash into the rehab ordeal.

city, but the trip will be well worth the effort. Try the grilled ham-and-cheese sandwich or the half-pound burger special. They're both winners and come with fries for under $4.50. If you don't happen to have a gold tooth or a tattoo of your ex-girlfriend on your arm, you may feel a bit out of place among the regulars. But don't let that scare you off. Sure, the rough-and-ready crowd at Riverside might look like they just finished working the carnival at the local parish picnic, but they're a friendly lot and always on the lookout for a party.

Java Express
10701 S. Hale Ave., Chicago
773/233-8557 Rating: \\\

The Rock Island line passes alongside this Beverly coffee shop, known for its excellent joe and sandwiches. A full sandwich ($5.50) will fill your belly, but not empty your wallet. I recommend a half sandwich and soup. It's more than enough. While you're at it, grab a milk or a pop for yourself. Six bucks will cover the cost. The bread and rolls

Drive a few blocks west and take a drive along nearby Longwood Drive or Seeley Avenue from 107th to 99th and check out the lovely mansions, mini-mansions, and architectural styles the neighborhood offers. If you're a Frank Lloyd Wright fan, you'll find several houses laid out by the master. Check with the Ridge Historical Society (773/881-1675, 10621 S. Seeley) for more information.

at Java are always fresh and tasty, and the tuna melt will bring the word *excellent* to your lips. Take your time as you eat. See how many trains you can count as they fly past. You might also want to jump in on a game of chess, checkers, or backgammon when your meal is over. At Java, game players are often lurking in the shadows, waiting to claim their next victim.

The BBQ Patio
3256 S. Ashland Ave., Chicago
773/523-7775   Rating: \\\

The many offerings at The BBQ Patio make it worth the trip. Grab a Greek salad, or a steak sandwich, or a gyro. This place is just a few biscuit flips away from several Streets and San yards so there are always plenty of over-sized men dropping $5-$7 on the counter for their meals, as well as hunks of food onto their laps. But don't let these sloppy fools offend you. They're not intentionally trying to spoon gravy and grilled onions onto their shirts and pants. They simply can't help themselves. Heed this advice: Eat your meal with proper manners and complete decorum. Remember, you are setting an example. We Streets and San men are nothing if not projects in the making, and we're constantly watching others to see how normal folks do things. Who knows? Maybe one day we might just get things right. Until then our brides will have to continue to wash the gravy stains from our flannel shirts and work pants.

Leif's
10350 S. Torrence Ave., Chicago
773/768-1859   Rating: \\\

Up until a year or so ago, if you grabbed a dictionary and looked up the words *greasy spoon*, in addition to the definition, you would no doubt have found a photograph or sketch of Leif's. However, that has all changed. Though Leif's is one of my favorite brunch spots, the owners recently gave the place a complete makeover, and in doing so I feel as if part of me has died. Gone are the old, beat-up booths and the old counter, both of which had the feel of long-lost friends. Gone is the old chalkboard upon which the daily specials were scribbled. At the old Leif's, you'd never find a menu. Now, a huge menu board, featuring a multitude of food options, hangs from the ceiling.

Although Leif's has changed its look, fortunately two things remain unchanged. Regardless of what you order, be it a Denver omelette or a hamburger, what you'll get is a large sampling of quality food, and it will definitely be greasy. Ah yes, big helpings and grease. I'm sure glad Leif's hasn't changed that. The food here has always been tasty, but you may want to pat it down first with a paper towel or two before you take your first bite. If you can't find any paper towels, you can always use your t-shirt, or you might consider sliding one of your socks off and putting it to use. I've done that before. The Streets and San Man is nothing, if not resourceful.

Capt'n Nemo's
3650 N. Ashland Ave., Chicago
773/929-SOUP   Rating: \\\

After you push through the door to Nemo's, you must, and I do mean must, get a sub and a soup. As for the subs, pick your poison. Though I'm partial to the South Sea (ham, salami, cheese, eggs, lettuce, tomato, onions, secret sauce, and pineapple sauce), every sub on the menu is excellent. As for the soups, split pea is offered every day, and an additional one is always available (Navy Bean—Monday; Hearty Barley—Tuesday; Minestrone—Wednesday; Lentil—Thursday; Vegetable—Friday). For a five spot, you can get half a sub and soup. Bigger appetites should get the whole sub for an extra three bucks.

Other Nemo locations:

- 7367 N. Clark St.
  Chicago
  773/973-0570

- 205 W. Dundee Rd.
  Buffalo Grove
  847/419-SOUP

- 38 N. Green Bay Rd.
  Winnetka
  847/446-6406

Smokin' Woody's
4160 N. Lincoln Ave., Chicago
773/880-1100   Rating: \\\

When the urge for a good pulled-pork sandwich comes and I find myself on the North Side, Smokin' Woody's is my stopping spot. For under $6, you'll get a quality sandwich, slaw, and fries or a baked potato. Should you decide

to stray from the pulled pork, they also offer several other top-quality sandwiches (chicken, $6.95; and brisket, $5.95). And, hey, why not try a side-order of the barbeque spaghetti ($2.50) just for kicks? It's guaranteed to be different from any spaghetti you've tasted before. Plenty of nice trinkets are hanging from the wall to give the feel of yesteryear, so go ahead and stare away if you're into that sort of thing. As for me, I'm simply here for the Que. It rates up there with the best in the area.

Illinois Bar & Grill
4135 W. 47th St., Chicago
773/847-2525   **Rating:** \\\\\

For a burger as big as a well-developed butt, Illinois B & G is the place for you. One-half pound of meat on a huge bun with lots of sloppy extras is what you get here. For $4.25, they'll throw the burger at you with a healthy heaping of fries. With every bite you take, your burger will slide from one side of the bun to the other. Tell me that doesn't sound like a great way to spend an afternoon. You may want to schedule an angioplasty with the medicine man after eating here.

Additional location:

• 1421 W. Taylor St.
  Chicago
  312/666-6666

Medici's
1327 E. 57th St., Chicago
773/667-7394
Rating: \\\

This quaint U. of C. eatery boasts good pizza, salads, and assorted sandwiches at reasonable prices. The spicy, grilled chicken sandwich will put a bit of starch in your collar, though it's a bit pricey at $8.00. Bring a Sharpie with you when you enter, and feel free to scribble your thoughts on the walls alongside those of the great U. of C. minds of the past. If you keep your eyes open you might even find a few bits of wisdom from yours truly on those walls. No, I didn't graduate from U. of C., but still, there's no doubting the fact that mine is a great mind.

DETOUR As long as you're here, take a walk or drive through the university area and take in some of the scenery. I must confess that when I'm on a college campus, I generally do a fair amount of girl watching. But not here. No way. Not at U. of C. What you'll see here won't exactly make your eyes dance. That being the case, take in some of the other, more interesting sights. The Robie House at 5757 S. Woodlawn by Frank Lloyd Wright always provides some interesting perspectives. Better yet, walk to and into the Rockefeller Chapel at 59th and Woodlawn. This famous house of worship is a pleasure to look at, and the interior woodwork is unbelievable, especially near the altar. Several great bookstores (57th Street Books, at 1301 E. 57th and The Seminary Co-Op Bookstore, at 5757 S. University) can also be found nearby.

Taste of Heaven
5401 N. Clark St., Chicago
773/989-0151   Rating: \\\½

When you push through the door to Taste of Heaven, you'll know right off that owner Dan McCauley has poured his heart and soul into this place. Family photos and delicate touches adorn the walls. And that's just dandy. But I don't come here just to stare at the walls. Hell, no. Danny Boy puts together several huge and tasty sandwiches ($7-8.95) as well as a knockout chicken pot pie for just under $8. These sandwiches are a bit pricier than most, but they're definitely worth a try. When you eat one, you'll get the feeling that you're not so much eating a sandwich as you are experiencing a work of art. And don't leave without taking a cake home with you. They're all excellent.

Maria's Gourmet Subs
1559 W. Devon Ave., Chicago
773/743-9900   Rating: \\\

Inside this little sub shop, you'll find several old black-and-white photos of Maria. She looks like a nice enough lady, even though she's holding back on the smile and all. All I know is this: if this woman was my mother and she offered the same food at home that she does in her sub shop, I'd be up in the 400-pound range right now, instead of the rather svelte 215 pounds I currently carry. And when Maria call her subs "gourmet," she means it. All sandwiches ($3.69) come on a good-sized hunk of baked torpedo bread lathered in a balsamic vinaigrette—the perfect tongue candy for starters. Add a healthy wedge of romaine lettuce, red onion, sliced cucumber, and a meat of any sort, and you have a wonderful, healthy sandwich. The hot, homemade meatloaf is my favorite.

Fireside Restaurant
5739 N. Ravenswood Ave., Chicago
773/878-5942   **Rating:** 〰〰〰

My reasons for coming to this restaurant are two-fold. Sure, they serve up quality pizza, ribs, and sandwiches in a friendly, neighborhood environment. Fireside has always been a place where I feel like I can eat and relax and whittle away some time. Grab a stool on the bar-side, say hello to Josh the bartender, and order a sandwich to your liking. Both the marinated steak sandwich ($7.95) and the bacon BBQ chicken sandwich ($6.95) will make your stomach stand up and applaud. Or, if you prefer, share a "za" with a friend, or toss back a half slab of wet ribs. The

DETOUR Rosehill Cemetery, one of Chicago's oldest spots for planting its dead, is directly across the street from Fireside. Go ahead and call me a cemetery nut. I confess; I am. I love old cemeteries because they keep me in touch with the past. Take a drive through Rosehill and you will come across numerous gravesites dating back to the early 1800s, and you'll find plot after plot of Chicago's rich and famous. Feel free to check in with the helpful staff at the entrance should you have a particular name you'd like to hunt down.

lunches are solid. My second reason is the nearby detour.

Fat Johnnies
7242 S. Western Ave., Chicago
773/737-6294   **Rating: **

This hot dog shack stands out among all the new and used car lots on Western Avenue because there's always a line of hungry, loyal hotdog fanatics waiting to order one of the best dogs in the city. When it comes to dogs, Johnnie does it right. He starts out with a scrumdillyicious steamed bun, a solid David Berg dog, and then he adds the extras: mustard, onion, relish, tomatoes, cukes, and celery salt. Make sure you order more than one dog, because you'll definitely want another after you eat the first. The dog ($1.50) gets top billing here, and rightly so, but there are several other good items on the menu. Want a bowl of tomatoes, cukes, and sauce? How about The Mother-In-Law, a tamale on a bun soaked in chili? Fat Johnnies has it all.

The Skinny on Fat Johnnies:

A Hot Dog a Day Helps Keep the Doctor Away

Sure, the experts and other assorted medicine men will tell you to stay away from hotdogs. They'll moan about the fat content of the dog itself and its lack of nutritional value. But what do they know? I'd rather listen to Fat Johnnies owner, John Pawlikowski, who opened his hot dog stand in 1972.

"I've eaten a hot dog every day of my life for over 30

years, and I'll tell you this. My cholesterol level is perfect, and my blood pressure is perfect, and I'm 55 years old."

A big man with an infectious laugh, John first entered the fast-food world in 1968 when he rolled a pushcart out to the corner of 69th and Damen.

"I bought a hot dog cart for $100 off a guy named Alex. See, I had a job over at the Nabisco plant at the time, but the truck drivers all went on strike and so the plant closed down. I had to find something to do. That's when I ran into Alex. I kept that cart going on the corner for 2–3 years, and then my dad gave us the lot on Western."

John, and his brother, Frank, ran Fat Johnnies together for over 15 years. Frank opened a second Fat Johnnies out in Orland Park and ran that place until he passed away seven years ago.

John's not shy when it comes to his hot dog views. "Nobody makes a better hot dog than me. Nobody. I make the best. Everything I have is fresh. Every day we make everything fresh. And we don't put ketchup on our dogs. Not unless they ask for it. But South Siders don't ask for ketchup. North Siders do."

"I originated the chili-cheese dog, too," John claimed. "Back in '72. Nobody had a chili-cheese dog back then. Now they all have it, but I still make the best."

Not much has changed at Fat Johnnies. The original 1972 menu is still posted like a sentry on the front. Sure, the prices have been painted over during the passage of years, but all the menu items are still the same, including the chili-cheese dog. John considered adding a deep fryer to make french fries at one time, but he has resisted the idea. "This place was built on the concept of a hot dog cart. We wanted to keep it simple. Sure, we have more room in here, but essentially we're still a pushcart. And I like it that way."

There is a certain beauty in simplicity, and the area people who have been flocking to Fat Johnnies for years will certainly agree. But the allure of Fat Johnnies goes far beyond the area. "People come to my place from all over. My furthest customer comes from England. There's a pub in England that has a picture of my place on the wall."

> There's a certain pride that jumps from John's mouth when he talks about his business and his products, and rightly so. When John dresses up his final dog, his son will take over the business. And what then for John? "I'm gonna head down to Key West, and I'm gonna fish everyday." ■

These Big Dogs Have Bite

Sure, Fat Johnnies serves up one of the best dogs around, but, as we all know, there are many other great dog joints in the area. To state it lightly—Chicago is definitely a hot dog town. Many a scribe has written about the best dog joints in our fair city, so I won't seek to reproduce that here. However, I will list a few of my favorite dog houses.

Now let's get one thing straight from the start concerning hot dogs: a good dog starts with the frank itself. Without a suitable, tasty frank, I don't care what you smother it with; it just doesn't meet the specifications of the Streets and San Man. However, if the frank is good, then bring on the extras. Load me up with mustard, onion, relish, tomatoes, cukes, dill pickle, sport peppers, and celery salt.

And please don't say: "What about the ketchup?" If you want ketchup on your dog, then you are ruining one of the great pleasures of our lifetime—the Chicago dog. The next thing you know, you'll probably want to put lights on the park at Wrigley. Oh yeah, someone already did that.

The places below do the dog justice. Some put a variety of different things on the dog, but the fact remains, they're all good.

- Bowser Dog
  4504 W. Irving Park Rd.
  Chicago
  773/282-8662

- Byron's
  680 N. Halsted St.
  Chicago
  312/738-0011

and

- 1017 W. Irving Park Rd.
  Chicago

- Dan's Hot Dogs
  9314 S. Ashland
  Chicago
  773/779-9123

- Demon Dogs
  944 W. Fullerton
  Chicago
  773/281-2001

- Don's Dogs
  7748 S. Kedzie Ave.
  Chicago
  773/476-9392

- Hot Dog Lady
  37th and Parnell Ave.
  Northwest Corner
  Chicago

- Janson's
  9900 S. Western Ave.
  Chicago
  773/238-3612

- O'Malley's
  3501 S. Union Ave.
  Chicago
  773/247-2700

- Wiener Circle
  2622 N. Clark St.
  Chicago
  773/477-7444

- Wolfy's
  2734 W. Peterson Ave.
  Chicago
  773/743-0207

- Red's
  formerly at 111th and
  Artesian
  Chicago
  Rest in Peace

Chi Tung
9560 S. Kedzie Ave., Evergreen Park
708/636-8180 Rating: \\\\\

Just on the outskirts of Chicago, Chi Tung offers a Chinese extravaganza at lunch. For $5.99, this all-you-can-eat buffet starts with soup and egg rolls and continues with excellent dishes that change every day of the week. Plan to spend some time. You want to ensure you fill yourself to the bursting point, and it's not hard to do with the likes of crab rangoon, shrimp-fried rice, chicken wings, Singapore chow mein, vegetable tempura, beef kow, tofu, and sweet and sour chicken—just to name a few. If you happen to have your kids with you, drag them in. For a measly $3.50 each, they can eat and ruin your meal—if they're like mine. Squabbling, always squabbling.

A & P Deli
704 S. Wabash Ave., Chicago
312/697-0283 Rating: \\\\

So maybe you just drove down to the South Loop for a Bears game and you're like me—you don't want to pay full price for a parking spot at Soldier Field. No one likes to have a gun held to their head, right? Well, as you search for a parking spot over on Wabash or Michigan Avenues, make sure you swing by this little deli to snatch a corned beef ($6.39) sandwich. There are several A & P Delis in the area, as well as lunch trucks. You can't go wrong. The sandwiches are a full pound and always served hot. I can just picture my old Irish grandfather's eyes light up if he ever saw a sandwich like this. Gramps has been dead for many,

many years, but a sandwich like this just might make a corned-beef lover like him claw his way up out of his grave.

La Pasadita
1132 N. Ashland Ave., Chicago
773/384-6537   Rating: ♦♦♦½

On Ashland near Division, you'll find three La Pasadita restaurants within 50 feet of each other (1132, 1140, and 1141 North Ashland), and all of them offer what just might be the best burrito in the city. Now, that's a bold statement to make, because as we all know, Chicago has many great burrito joints. Try it and see if the Streets and San Man speaks the truth. Order a steak burrito and make certain you have them include the roasted jalapeño pepper sauce, as well as all of the other standard ingredients (cilantro, onion, and cheese). The sauce is what makes the burrito, and it will give you a new appreciation for Mexican food. Toss a pop into the mix, and all you'll drop in this place is a fin.

Mama Nena's Shrimphouse
1623 W. 43rd St., Chicago
773/254-9380   Rating: ♦♦♦½

Walk into this shrimp house and do what comes naturally. Let your nose sniff away at the delicious scents sailing through the air. Then order a pound of these puppies and go to your car, van, or truck and eat. Sure, there are plenty of seats available at Mama Nena's, but if you eat your meal inside your vehicle, that lovely shrimp smell will remain there for two to three days. Then you can feel as if you're enjoying that shrimp again, again, and again. Ah yes, Mama Nena's is to die for. The jumbo shrimp will come at over $10 a pound, but they're well worth the price. Personally, the medium shrimp at $7 a pound more than takes care of my shrimp needs. You can order a meal that comes with fries and bread, or you can get one of the other fish specials of the day.

Carmen's
6568 N. Sheridan Rd., Chicago
773/465-1700   Rating: ﹩﹩﹩

Just a spit away from Loyola University, this eatery offers one of the absolute best bargain buffets in the city. Feel like some soup, salad, pizza, pasta, pop, and dessert? Feel like some more soup, salad, pizza, pasta, pop, and dessert? At Carmens, for $5.95, you can eat as much as you'd like and refill your pop glass as many times as you desire. Droves of co-eds flock to this joint, and they keep the place hopping with their lively chit-chat. Plenty of seating is available, so bring all the troops to cash in on this bargain.

Take a walk through Loyola's campus. One of the premier Catholic Universities in the area, there are many interesting buildings to see and explore. If you're not up for a campus jaunt, walk a few blocks further north and stop in The Armadillo's Pillow (6753 N. Sheridan Rd., 773/761-2558), a quaint used bookstore with an excellent stock of books.

The Soup Box
2943 N. Broadway St., Chicago
773/935-9800   **Rating:** \\\

How's about a good soup and some tasty sourdough bread and butter to go with it. That's what we Streets and San guys call eating light. If you're north, the Soup Box is definitely the place for you. It serves a wide variety of soups year round. In the colder months, Soup Box offers over 20 varieties of soups, including split pea, potato leek, and lobster bisque, just to name a few. In summer, the Soup Box turns its face south and unloads most of the soups in favor of huge, slushy-type drinks. They still, however, offer up four soups for the asking. So, even on a 95-degree day you can get soup and eat it in the comfort of your well air-conditioned auto. Just watch the steam roll out of the soup container and wrestle with the AC as you slurp ever so slowly. That's livin', I'm telling you.

Gio's
2724 S. Lowe Ave., Chicago
312/225-6368   **Rating:** \\\½

This tiny, neighborhood store takes care of the local residents with good cold cuts and other Italian dishes at lunch. Plant yourself at one of the few tables and order the chicken vesuvio sandwich or go with the linguine and clam sauce. All the meals on the menu are reasonably priced ($3 to $7) and guaranteed to fill you up. The paisans in this place are as plentiful as the bags of pasta on the shelves, so don't be offended if people keep trying to hug you every few seconds or so, or if they look like they just left the set of *The Sopranos*. Excellent bread, cheese, and oil are delivered promptly upon your arrival, so you can stretch your stomach as you await the main course.

Hot Tip from Tony the Hat:

The Full Package

So maybe you're heading to a day game over at U.S. Cellular Field, or maybe you simply find yourself in the Bridgeport area around noon. In either situation, your tum-tum is in desperate need of some quality chow. You don't want just any old meal. No, you want some grub that you can savor and then, later, brag to your friends about. If that's the case, take this advice from Tony "the Hat" Bertucci.

"Gio's has the best hot sandwiches in the city. Try the chicken parm or the chicken vesuvio sandwich. They're both excellent."

A lifelong Bridgeporter, Tony walks the walk and talks the talk of those who belong to the neighborhood that has produced more Chicago mayors than any other neighborhood. Known for the dapper black hat he wears in the winter, and also for the never-ending supply of sleeveless T-shirts he wears in the summer, Tony knows where to direct people in and about his turf.

"You can't go wrong with any of the specials in Gio's," Tony says. "Try the lasagna, the linguine and clams; try any of 'em. They're all good. And the portions are more than generous." Tony cuts loose with a smile and then continues. "As for me, personally, I'll say this. Gio's chicken vesuvio sandwich is, bar none, the absolute best in the city. Just picture the wine and garlic sauce and the peas fallin' off the chicken and roll as you take a bite. It's the best. You hear me. The best."

Tony Bertucci: city electrician, precinct captain, husband, father of two, food critic, adviser to the stars. This guy's the whole package and then some. Heed his advice. Try any of the specials from Gio's and you'll thank him. As a matter of fact, if you go to Gio's, you'll probably find Tony there. He'll be one of those Italians I warned you about; you know—the ones who are always trying to give you a hug. ■

The Shelter Deli
605 E. 87th St., Chicago
773/487-1550   Rating: \\\

This tiny, corned-beef hut is a must for your list. There are many different sandwiches you can get here, but the corned beef ($5.09) is mammoth and made with fall-off-the-bone meat. Wash it down with a couple of hot peppers and a coke and you will certainly feel like a champ. The folks who work the counter always seem to be in the midst of some ongoing argument, so your sandwich wait-time will usually be peppered with some interesting thoughts, if you catch my drift. This joint is a mere six blocks from the Dan Ryan exit at 87th Street, so you can always get here in a hurry.

Bacci Pizzeria
2248 W. Taylor St., Chicago
312/455-9000   Rating: \\\

With several Bacci shops around, you're never far away from a great pizza deal. You can order a variety of food items from the menu, but this joint is known for their Pizza and Pop special for $3. The folks at Bacci don't skimp when it comes to size. The pizza slice you receive will be big enough to eat with both hands. There are some

who say you can cover an entire Ford Escort with it, but that might be a bit of an exaggeration. In any event, Bacci is the perfect place for the poor man's lunch.

A couple other Bacci locations:

- 5004 S. Archer Ave.
  Chicago
  773/585-4400

- 120 N. Wells St.
  Chicago
  312/782-0000

Hagen's Fish Market
5635 W. Montrose Ave., Chicago
773/283-1944   Rating: ♨♨♨

This Northwest-side fishery has been a staple in the neighborhood for years and years. Order a pound of the jumbo shrimp, or have a half-pound if you want to take it

DETOUR → As long as you're less than two miles away, you should stop at the Chicagoland Canoe Base at 4019 N. Narragansett—sure to delight the eye of anyone, even if you're not into canoeing or kayaking. Eye the many canoes, kayaks, and accessories. There's also a huge assortment of magazines and books that offer great ideas for family camping, hiking, and canoe trips. In back, you'll discover hundreds of kayaks and canoes for rent, and you can also see several huge (40-feet plus) Viking-type boats that owner Ralph Frieze and his staff are working on. The staff is extremely helpful, so fire away with questions.

easy. For $7, you can get a half-pound of shrimp, fries, and a pop. A huge selection of other fish is available. Go for some talapia, or scallops, or maybe you have the feel for some calamari. They'll cook any fish you select and make a sandwich of it. You can bring your own catch to Hagen's as well, and they'll smoke it to perfection for you. Hagen's is your full-service fish market.

T's Tap
9801 S. Ewing Ave., Chicago
773/221-3111   **Rating:** \\\\\

Sure there's a back room, but the bar itself is barely big enough to serve a meal to Jesus and his 12 Disciples. But that's part of the beauty of T's Tap. When you put a gathering into a smallish room, they have to talk. And at T's, believe me when I say this, the people here (owners, bartenders, cooks, and patrons) talk and talk and talk. Everyone knows everyone in this joint. "Hello's," "how ya doin's," and quick stories fly out of every mouth. Even if you're an outsider, you won't feel like one—you'll be treated nice and quickly brought into the mix. And the food—ah, yes, the food. T's Tap doesn't get four forks for nothing. For starters, try any of the soups. For $1.50, they're filling and tasty. The stuffed green pepper soup is one of the best in Chicago. Whenever I eat it, I skip down the sidewalk like a second-grader. It's that good. The standard fare is burgers, boneless pork chops, sausage, Bar-Be-Que Beef, and so on. All the meals are excellent and are priced under $5. This is another joint for your don't miss list.

Parnell Foods
3642 S. Parnell Ave., Chicago
773/373-2688 **Rating:** \\\\

If you drive along the 3600 block of Parnell in the early morning or at lunch, you'll find the street clogged with doubled-parked Streets and San vans and trucks, and you'll see hordes of big-bellied men marching in and out of Parnell Foods. Owner Donna Winge, along with her staff of friendly women, offer excellent soups for $2.25-$2.75, and her sandwiches are always ready to be inhaled.

At the northwest corner of 37th and Parnell, you'll find "the Hot Dog Lady," as my kids call her. Once the baseball season starts, Kathy DeCarlo sets up her dog stand and runs it from roughly 4–10 P.M. Her hot dog is one of the absolute best in the entire city. I'd give the Hot Dog Lady a review of her own, but she's not around until well after lunch (except on weekends), so she doesn't exactly meet my lunch-time criterion. Nonetheless, this place is certainly worthy of a mention. Should you find yourself here for a Sox game, or if you just want to cruise by for a great dog, give this place a shot. Order everything (mustard, relish, onion, tomatoes, sport peppers, giardiniera, and cukes) on your dog and see how your mouth feels. I live 10 miles from this joint and still drive in with my kids for a dog every now and again on a Saturday afternoon. It's well worth the trip.

If rubbing up against the big bellies of my cohorts as you squeeze your way down the aisles of this tiny store doesn't offend you, you'll experience the good chow and the Bridgeport atmosphere for yourself. You're within sight of U.S. Cellular ballpark, so don't be bold and talk about the Cubs. If you do, you might just get a tongue-lashing from a nearby sox fan.

Frank's Chicago Shrimp House
10410 S. Kedzie Ave., Chicago
773/445-3100   Rating: ♦♦♦½

Open for just shy of a year, this Southwest Side shrimp house has already made a huge impact with the locals. The lunch crowd here lines up for several varieties of shrimp—and they're all good—but try my favorite, the Chicago style, where the deep-fried prawns are covered with a batter lightly seasoned to perfection. Owner Julie Moore and her staff are courteous and quick, and that's one heck of a combo these days, if I do say so myself. Grab a dinner and you'll get a half-pound of shrimp, fries, and slaw for $7.50. Toss a pop in to soothe your throat and the damage will be just over $8.00. If you can spare a few more one-spots, give the hush puppies (10 for $1.95) a whirl. You won't regret it. There's plenty of seating available, and if you choose to eat in, you can enjoy your shrimp as you watch the Kedzie Avenue foot traffic march by.

Other Frank's Shrimp House locations:

- 4459 S. Archer Ave.
  Chicago
  773/523-4624

- 5439 W. Addison St.
  Chicago
  773/286-2533

De Angelos Deli
808 N. State St., Chicago
312/943-3354   Rating: \\\

The steak sandwich ($5.40 for an eight-incher), dressed up with onions and cheese and a tasty mixture of spices, is a definite winner. The tuna boat is also one of my favorites. Order one of these subs or grab some pasta or whatever the heck else you want, but whatever you do, make certain you get a soup. Whatever the soup of the day is at De Angelos—get it. These luscious mixtures are always great and packed full of veggies, meats, noodles, and whatever else was lying on the counter the night before. This is soup the way your grandmother made it.

Stan's Drive-in
3001 S. Archer Ave., Chicago
773/376-0198   Rating: \\\

This bright yellow shack sits like a beacon on Archer Avenue and kicks out good breakfast food, soups, and fast food on a regular basis. The hot dog special (dog, fries, and a small Coke) is the poor man's special at $2.50. However, my recommendation is the Thursday special—Sloppy Joes for $2. Ah, yes, these Joes are just like the kind my Uncle Kilty used to make. They're big, bountiful, and have just the right spices. Give it a try. Make my Uncle Kilty proud. Who knows? After eating two of these Joes, you might feel like dancing an Irish jig. That's what Kilty liked to do after he devoured one of his own Joes. Of course, he usually had a wee bit of whiskey in him as well.

The Time Has Come To Say Goodbye

Thanks a mint for buying this book and giving it a thorough read. I hope you get the chance to visit many of the eateries contained herein, and I hope you enjoy them—as well as the nearby detours—as much as I have. If you happen to make it to every eatery in this book, let me know how much weight you put on during the course of the adventure. As a final token of my appreciation, I have a few parting gifts for you. Put them to good use, and make sure you get your money's worth out of the enclosed coupons.

The Streets and San Man's Top 25 List

1. Best Italian sub: . . . . .Bari Foods

2. Best meatball sandwich: . . . . .Beggar's Pizza

3. Best place to watch a family squabble: . . . . .Lincoln Tavern

4. Best place to watch the world pass by: . . . . .Wikstrom's Deli

5. Best sloppy sub: . . . . .Fontano's Subs

6. Best place to catch an Irish brogue: . . . . .Emerald Isle

7. Best burger bargain: . . . . .Nicky's

8. Best place to get that "at the beach feeling": . . . . .Crabby Kim's

9. Best pizza: . . . . .Vito and Nick's

10. Best place to see a smorgasbord of tattoos: . . . . . . .Riverside Marina

11. Best hot dog: . . . . .Fat Johnnies

12. Best place to overeat: . . . . .Fogo de Chao

13. Best pub grub: . . . . .Frank and Mary's

14. Best place to smoke a fish: . . . . .Hagen's Fish Market

15. Best Sloppy Joe: . . . . .Stan's

16. Best burrito: . . . . .La Pasadita

17. Second-best place to catch an Irish brogue: . . .Murray's Pub & Grill

18. Best shrimp: . . . . .Mama Nena's

19. Best place to watch the trains go by: . . . . .Java Express

20. Best Que: . . . . .Chuck's BBQ

21. Best detour after a meal: .The Douglas tomb

22. Best soup: . . . . .Casino Restaurant

23. Best place to steal a set of teeth: . . . . .Arch-View

24. Best breaded steak sandwich: .La Milanese

25. Second-best detour after a meal: . . . . .Big Chief

The Perfect Day

For the typical Streets and San guy, lunch is, as we all know by now, definitely the focal point of the day. However, there may be times when you (the reader) really get hit with huge hunger pangs; days when your stomach seems to rule your mind; days when all you can hear are these words coming from your subconscious: "I need food. I need food." On such days, you might have to snag a quick breakfast sandwich to start the day, grab your usual lunch, and then, at day's end, you might feel the need to wolf down a dog to cap things off. Who knows? A bedtime snack might even be required to get you ready for snooze time. If I had my perfect (dream) day, I'd do the following:

Breakfast:

- Stevie G's
  3558 S. Ashland Ave.
  Chicago
  773/376-3794

This eatery is the home of the mondo breakfast sub. There's nothing quite like starting the day off with a nice foot-long hunk of French bread upon which the cook will deposit three eggs, three slices of bacon, three sausages, some ham, and mozzarella cheese for a paltry $4.25. If this meal doesn't make your morning engine purr, nothing will.

Lunch:

Hit any eatery in this here book.

End-of-the-workday snack:

It's time to grab a dog with the works from The Hot Dog Lady at 37th and Parnell (See the detour on page 86 for the full scoop on the Hot Dog Lady). Her 4 P.M. opening time makes this a great stopping place when returning to your workplace or while returning home at the end of the day. And hey, since she's close to the Dan Ryan expressway, you can always zip in and zip out in a matter of minutes.

Bed-time snack:

Oftentimes at the end of a long day, I find myself all worn out from the job and from the little beasts (children) that my wife makes me entertain when I get home. Just before I put on my jammies and climb into bed, I like to reward myself with some much-needed nourishment.

Here are my two favorite bed-time snacks:

1. The Streets and San Man's BLTCE&G (This is a Bacon, Lettuce, Tomato, Cheese, Egg, and Giardiniera sandwich.) For the specifics on this luscious sandwich, please see page 45. Sure, this sandwich can be used to pump energy into your system, but when I'm in dire need of rest, it will hit my stomach like a rock and push me off to snooze-land in a manner of minutes.

2. Peanut Butter and Jelly Pancake. Cook a large pancake in a big pan and brown both sides lightly to perfection. Feel free to drop a few blueberries or

chocolate morsels into the pancake should you so desire. Smother one side of the cooked pancake with peanut butter while the pancake is still hot, so that the peanut butter gets all gooey and soft, and then top it with some jelly. Fold this contraption in half and eat it as a sandwich, or leave it on your plate and cut it up as you would an omelet. Yee-hah! This simple snack is definite proof that PB&J sandwiches aren't just for kids.

CONTACT THE STREETS AND SAN MAN

Put your Perfect Day together and let me know about it. Also, I'm always looking for more good off-the-beaten-track lunch joints to visit. You can e-mail me at streetsandsanman@sbcglobal.net to tell me about your favorite joints and to let me know what you think about mine. By the way, did you know I'm also an advice columnist? Well it's the truth. Someone had to pick up where Ann Landers left off, right? Feel free to forward your questions or tales of woe to me, and I'll get right back to you. I know my stuff when it comes to food, but as you can assuredly tell by now, I'm a lot more worldly than that. I know a lot about a lot, and we'll leave it at that. Good-bye.

COUPONS

Clip a coupon from the following pages and bring it to the eatery for a $1 discount. As advertised, with the use of these coupons, this book will more than pay for itself.

The bearer of this coupon is entitled to a
$1 discount with a purchase of $10 or more at

BACCI PIZZERIA
$1.00 off

Expires 12-31-2006
Coupon taken from *The Streets and San Man's Guide to Chicago Eats*

- -

The bearer of this coupon is entitled to a
$1 discount with a purchase of $10 or more at

BARI FOODS
$1.00 off

Expires 12-31-2006
Coupon taken from *The Streets and San Man's Guide to Chicago Eats*

- -

The bearer of this coupon is entitled to a
$1 discount with a purchase of $10 or more at

BEGGAR'S PIZZA
$1.00 off

Expires 12-31-2006
Coupon taken from *The Streets and San Man's Guide to Chicago Eats*

- -

The bearer of this coupon is entitled to a
$1 discount with a purchase of $10 or more at

THE BRICK AND BEAM PUB
$1.00 off

Expires 12-31-2006
Coupon taken from *The Streets and San Man's Guide to Chicago Eats*

The Streets and San Man's Guide to Chicago Eats

The Streets and San Man's Guide to Chicago Eats

The Streets and San Man's Guide to Chicago Eats

The Streets and San Man's Guide to Chicago Eats

The bearer of this coupon is entitled to a
$1 discount with a purchase of $10 or more at

CARMEN'S
$1.00 off

Expires 12-31-2006
Coupon taken from *The Streets and San Man's Guide to Chicago Eats*

The bearer of this coupon is entitled to a
$1 discount with a purchase of $10 or more at

D.A.'S DELI
$1.00 off

Expires 12-31-2006
Coupon taken from *The Streets and San Man's Guide to Chicago Eats*

The bearer of this coupon is entitled to a
$1 discount with a purchase of $10 or more at

DE ANGELOS DELI
$1.00 off

Expires 12-31-2006
Coupon taken from *The Streets and San Man's Guide to Chicago Eats*

The bearer of this coupon is entitled to a
$1 discount with a purchase of $10 or more at

FIRESIDE RESTAURANT
$1.00 off

Expires 12-31-2006
Coupon taken from *The Streets and San Man's Guide to Chicago Eats*

The Streets and San Man's Guide to Chicago Eats

The Streets and San Man's Guide to Chicago Eats

The Streets and San Man's Guide to Chicago Eats

The Streets and San Man's Guide to Chicago Eats

The bearer of this coupon is entitled to a
$1 discount with a purchase of $10 or more at

FONTANO'S SUBS
$1.00 off

Expires 12-31-2006
Coupon taken from *The Streets and San Man's Guide to Chicago Eats*

The bearer of this coupon is entitled to a
$1 discount with a purchase of $10 or more at

FRANK & MARY'S TAVERN
$1.00 off

Expires 12-31-2006
Coupon taken from *The Streets and San Man's Guide to Chicago Eats*

The bearer of this coupon is entitled to a
$1 discount with a purchase of $10 or more at

GRANT'S GRILL & GALLERY
$1.00 off

Expires 12-31-2006
Coupon taken from *The Streets and San Man's Guide to Chicago Eats*

The bearer of this coupon is entitled to a
$1 discount with a purchase of $10 or more at

GRIZZLY'S LODGE
$1.00 off

Expires 12-31-2006
Coupon taken from *The Streets and San Man's Guide to Chicago Eats*

The Streets and San Man's Guide to Chicago Eats

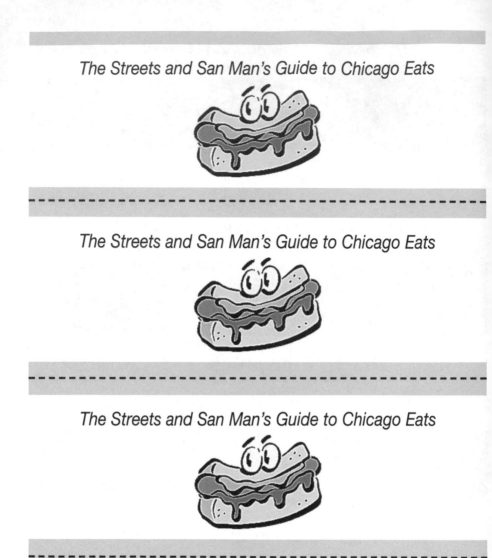

The Streets and San Man's Guide to Chicago Eats

The Streets and San Man's Guide to Chicago Eats

The Streets and San Man's Guide to Chicago Eats

The bearer of this coupon is entitled to a
$1 discount with a purchase of $10 or more at

JAVA EXPRESS
$1.00 off

Expires 12-31-2006
Coupon taken from *The Streets and San Man's Guide to Chicago Eats*

The bearer of this coupon is entitled to a
$1 discount with a purchase of $10 or more at

KINCADE'S
$1.00 off

Expires 12-31-2006
Coupon taken from *The Streets and San Man's Guide to Chicago Eats*

The bearer of this coupon is entitled to a
$1 discount with a purchase of $10 or more at

LALO'S
$1.00 off

Expires 12-31-2006
Coupon taken from *The Streets and San Man's Guide to Chicago Eats*

The bearer of this coupon is entitled to a
$1 discount with a purchase of $10 or more at

M & J'S LOUNGE
$1.00 off

Expires 12-31-2006
Coupon taken from *The Streets and San Man's Guide to Chicago Eats*

The Streets and San Man's Guide to Chicago Eats

The Streets and San Man's Guide to Chicago Eats

The Streets and San Man's Guide to Chicago Eats

The Streets and San Man's Guide to Chicago Eats

The bearer of this coupon is entitled to a
$1 discount with a purchase of $10 or more at

MICELI'S DELI
$1.00 off

Expires 12-31-2006
Coupon taken from *The Streets and San Man's Guide to Chicago Eats*

The bearer of this coupon is entitled to a
$1 discount with a purchase of $10 or more at

MURRAY'S PUB & GRILL
$1.00 off

Expires 12-31-2006
Coupon taken from *The Streets and San Man's Guide to Chicago Eats*

The bearer of this coupon is entitled to a
$1 discount with a purchase of $10 or more at

MY BOY JACK'S
$1.00 off

Expires 12-31-2006
Coupon taken from *The Streets and San Man's Guide to Chicago Eats*

The bearer of this coupon is entitled to a
$1 discount with a purchase of $10 or more at

NICKY'S
$1.00 off

Expires 12-31-2006
Coupon taken from *The Streets and San Man's Guide to Chicago Eats*

The Streets and San Man's Guide to Chicago Eats

The Streets and San Man's Guide to Chicago Eats

The Streets and San Man's Guide to Chicago Eats

The Streets and San Man's Guide to Chicago Eats

The bearer of this coupon is entitled to a
$1 discount with a purchase of $10 or more at

O'LEARY'S PUBLIC HOUSE
$1.00 off

Expires 12-31-2006
Coupon taken from *The Streets and San Man's Guide to Chicago Eats*

The bearer of this coupon is entitled to a
$1 discount with a purchase of $10 or more at

SAMMY'S COUNTRY KITCHIN
$1.00 off

Expires 12-31-2006
Coupon taken from *The Streets and San Man's Guide to Chicago Eats*

The bearer of this coupon is entitled to a
$1 discount with a purchase of $10 or more at

SMOKIN' WOODY'S
$1.00 off

Expires 12-31-2006
Coupon taken from *The Streets and San Man's Guide to Chicago Eats*

The bearer of this coupon is entitled to a
$1 discount with a purchase of $10 or more at

T'S TAP
$1.00 off

Expires 12-31-2006
Coupon taken from *The Streets and San Man's Guide to Chicago Eats*

The Streets and San Man's Guide to Chicago Eats

The Streets and San Man's Guide to Chicago Eats

The Streets and San Man's Guide to Chicago Eats

The Streets and San Man's Guide to Chicago Eats

*The bearer of this coupon is entitled to a
$1 discount with a purchase of $10 or more at*

VITO & NICK'S
$1.00 off

Expires 12-31-2006
Coupon taken from *The Streets and San Man's Guide to Chicago Eats*

 *The bearer of this coupon is entitled to a
$1 discount with a purchase of $10 or more at*

FRANK'S CHICAGO SHRIMP HOUSE
$1.00 off

Expires 12-31-2006
Coupon taken from *The Streets and San Man's Guide to Chicago Eats*

---

 *The bearer of this coupon is entitled to a
$1 discount with a purchase of $10 or more at*

LEIF'S
$1.00 off

Expires 12-31-2006
Coupon taken from *The Streets and San Man's Guide to Chicago Eats*

---

*The bearer of this coupon is entitled to a
$1 discount with a purchase of $10 or more at*

MAMA NENA'S SHRIMPHOUSE
$1.00 off

Expires 12-31-2006
Coupon taken from *The Streets and San Man's Guide to Chicago Eats*

The Streets and San Man's Guide to Chicago Eats

The Streets and San Man's Guide to Chicago Eats

The Streets and San Man's Guide to Chicago Eats

The Streets and San Man's Guide to Chicago Eats

INDEX

FOOD TYPES

Big Meals

Burgers

Chicken Sandwiches

Chinese

Corned Beef

Dogs

Hot Sandwiches

Italian

Itailan Beefs/Combo

Also from Lake Claremont Press...

Chicago Haunts: Ghostlore of the Windy City

More Chicago Haunts: Scenes from Myth and Memory

Creepy Chicago: A Ghosthunter's Tales of the City's Scariest Sites

Muldoon: A True Chicago Ghost Story: Tales of a Forgotten Rectory

Graveyards of Chicago: The People, History, Art, and Lore of Cook County Cemeteries

Haunted Michigan: Recent Encounters with Active Spirits

More Haunted Michigan: New Encounters with Ghosts of the Great Lakes State

Great Chicago Fires: Historic Blazes That Shaped a City

The Firefighter's Best Friend: Lives and Legends of Chicago Firehouse Dogs

Chicago's Midway Airport: The First Seventy-Five Years

The Chicago River: A Natural and Unnatural History

The Hoofs & Guns of the Storm: Chicago's Civil War Connections

Hollywood on Lake Michigan: 100 Years of Chicago and the Movies

"The Movies Are": Carl Sandburg's Film Reviews and Essays, 1920–1928

Literary Chicago: A Book Lover's Tour of the Windy City

Near West Side Stories: Struggles for Community in Chicago's Maxwell Street Neighborhood

A Cook's Guide to Chicago

A Native's Guide to Northwest Indiana

COMING SOON

A Native's Guide to Chicago, 4th Edition

The Golden Age of Chicago Children's Television

Finding Your Chicago Ancestors

The Politics of Place: A History of Zoning in Chicago

Wrigley Field's Last World Series: The Wartime Chicago Cubs and The Pennant of 1945

Chicago Haunts: Ghostlore of the Windy City
by Ursula Bielski
From ruthless gangsters to restless mail order kings, from the Fort Dearborn Massacre to the St. Valentine's Day Massacre, the phantom remains of the passionate people and volatile events of Chicago history have made the Second City second to none in the annals of American ghostlore. Bielski captures over 160 years of this haunted history with her distinctive blend of lively storytelling, in-depth historical research, exclusive interviews, and insights from parapsychology. Called "a masterpiece of the genre," "a must-read," and "an absolutely first-rate-book" by reviewers, Chicago Haunts continues to earn the praise of critics and readers alike.
0-9642426-7-2, October 1998, softcover, 277 pages, 29 photos, $15.00

More Chicago Haunts: Scenes from Myth and Memory
by Ursula Bielski
50 new stories! Step back inside "the biggest ghost town in America."
1-893121-04-6, October 2000, softcover, 312 pages, 50 photos, $15.00

Graveyards of Chicago: The People, History, Art, and Lore of Cook County Cemeteries
by Matt Hucke and Ursula Bielski
Ever wonder where Al Capone is buried? How about Clarence Darrow? Muddy Waters? Harry Caray? And what really lies beneath home plate at Wrigley Field? Graveyards of Chicago answers these and other cryptic questions as it charts the lore and lure of Chicago's ubiquitous burial grounds. Grab a shovel and tag along as Ursula Bielski and Matt Hucke unearth the legends and legacies that mark Chicago's silent citizens.
0-9642426-4-8, November 1999, softcover, 228 pages, 168 photos, $15.00

Haunted Michigan: Recent Encounters with Active Spirits
by Rev. Gerald S. Hunter
Within these pages you will not find ancient ghost stories or legendary accounts of spooky events of long ago. Instead, Rev. Hunter shares his investigations into modern ghost stories—active hauntings that continue to this day. Wherever you may dwell, these tales of Michigan's ethereal residents are sure to make you think about the possibility, as Hunter suggests, that we are not always alone within the confines of our happy homes.
1-893121-10-0, October 2000, softcover, 207 pages, 20 photos, $12.95

More Haunted Michigan: New Encounters with Ghosts of the Great Lakes State
by Rev. Gerald S. Hunter
Rev. Hunter invited readers of Haunted Michigan to open their minds to the presence of the paranormal all around them. They opened their mind...and unlocked a grand repository of their own personal supernatural experiences. Hunter investigated these modern, active hauntings and recounts the most chilling and most unusual here for you, in further confirmation that the Great Lakes State may be one of the most haunted places in the country.
1-893121-29-1, February 2003, softcover, 260 pages, 22 photos, $15.00

Creepy Chicago: A Ghosthunter's Tales of the City's Scariest Sites
by Ursula Bielski
Nineteen true tales of Chicago's famous phantoms, haunted history, and unsolved mysteries, for readers ages 8–12.
1-893121-15-1, August 2003, softcover, illustrations, glossary, bibliography, $8.00

Muldoon: A True Chicago Ghost Story: Tales of a Forgotten Rectory
by Rocco Facchini and Daniel Facchini
These are the untold stories of the last days of a forgotten Chicago parish by the last person able to tell them, delving into church history, clerical politics, local folklore, neighborhood sociology, and paranormal activity.
1-893121-24-0, September 2003, softcover, historic photos, illustrations, $15.00

REGIONAL HISTORY

Chicago's Midway Airport: The First Seventy-Five Years
by Christopher Lynch
Midway was Chicago's first official airport, and for decades it was the busiest airport in the nation, and then the world. Lynch captures the spirit of adventure of the dawn of flight, combining narrative, essays, and oral histories to tell the engrossing tale of Midway Airport and the evolution of aviation right along with it. Recommended by the Chicago Sun-Times.
1-893121-18-6, January 2003, softcover, 10" x 8", 201 pages, 205 historic and contemporary photos, $19.95

Great Chicago Fires: Historic Blazes That Shaped a City
by David Cowan

As Chicago changed from agrarian outpost to industrial giant, it would be visited time and again by some of the worst infernos in American history—fires that sparked not only banner headlines but, more importantly, critical upgrades in fire safety laws across the globe. Acclaimed author and veteran firefighter David Cowan tells the story of the other "great" Chicago fires, noting the causes, consequences, and historical context of each. In transporting readers beyond the fireline and into the ruins, Cowan brings readers up close to the heroism, awe, and devastation generated by the fires that shaped Chicago.
1-893121-07-0, August 2001, softcover, 10" x 8", 167 pages, 86 historic and contemporary photographs, $19.95

The Firefighter's Best Friend: Lives and Legends of Chicago Firehouse Dogs
by Trevor and Drew Orsinger

Working dogs are an often-overlooked segment of the canine population. The Firefighter's Best Friend provides a rare look into a specific type of these dogs—those who have lived or currently live in the firehouses of Chicago. The Orsinger brothers take readers on a tour of Chicago firehouses in their quest to document the lives and legends of every known Chicago firedog past and present. As seen in Dog & Kennel and Animal Fair magazines, and in the popular Dogs with Jobs television series.
1-893121-20-8, September 2003, softcover, 11" x 8.5", 163 pages, historic and contemporary photos, $19.95

The Hoofs and Guns of the Storm: Chicago's Civil War Connections
by Arnie Bernstein; foreword by Senator Paul Simon

While America's Civil War was fought on Confederate battlefields, Chicago played a crucial role in the Union's struggle toward victory. Take an in-depth tour of the 19th century people, places, and events that created the foundation for modern-day Chicago. Recommended by top Civil War historians. With a separate section on Chicago's Abraham Lincoln and Lincoln family history, four walking tours/maps, and 88 historic and contemporary photos and artifacts.
1-893121-2006-2, September 2003, softcover, 284 pages, $15.95

Hollywood on Lake Michigan: 100 Years of Chicago and the Movies
by Arnie Bernstein, foreword by Soul Food writer/director George Tillman, Jr.

Tours, trivia, special articles, historic and contemporary photos, film profiles, anecdotes, and exclusive interviews with dozens of personalities spotlight Chicago and Chicagoans' distinguished role in cinematic history. Winner of an American Regional History Publishing Award: 1st Place—Midwest, 2000.
0-9642426-2-1, December 1998, softcover, 364 pages, 80 photos, $15.00

A Cook's Guide to Chicago: Where to Find Everything You Need and Lots of Things You Didn't Know You Did
by Marilyn Pocius

Chef and food writer Marilyn Pocius's new book takes food lovers and serious home cooks into all corners of Chicagoland in her explorations of local foodways. In addition to providing extensive information on specialty food and equipment shops (including gourmet stores, health food shops, butchers, fishmongers, produce stands, spice shops, ethnic grocers, and restaurant supplies dealers), Pocius directs readers to farmers markets, knife sharpeners, foodie clubs, cooking classes, and culinary publications. Her special emphasis on what to do with the variety of unusual ingredients found in ethnic supermarkets includes "Top 10" lists, simple recipes, and tips on using exotic ingredients. A complete index makes it easy to find what you need: frozen tropical fruit pulp, smoked goat feet, fresh durian, sanding sugar, empanada dough, live, egusi seeds, mugwort flour, kishke, and over 2,000 other items you didn't know you couldn't live without!

1-893121-16-X, May 2002, softcover, 288 pages, recipes and walking tours, $15.00

A Native's Guide to Northwest Indiana
by Mark Skertic

At the southern tip of Lake Michigan, in the crook between Chicagoland and southwestern Michigan, lies Northwest Indiana, a region of natural diversity, colorful history, abundant recreational opportunities, small town activities, and urban diversions. Whether you're a life-long resident, new in the area, or just passing through, let native Mark Skertic be your personal tour guide of the best the region has to offer. With regional maps, chapters on 31 communities, and special sections on antiques, boating, gaming, golf courses, the lakeshore and dunes, shopping, theater, and more.

1-893121-08-9, August 2003, softcover, 319 pages, photos, maps, $15.00

A Native's Guide to Chicago, 4th Edition
Lake Claremont Press, ed. by Sharon Woodhouse

Venture into the nooks and crannies of everyday Chicago with this comprehensive budget guide to over hundreds of free, inexpensive, and unusual things to do in the Windy City. Named "Best Guidebook for Locals" in New City's 1999 "Best of Chicago" issue!

1-893131-23-2, Spring 2004, softcover, 400+ pages, maps, $15.95

ORDER FORM

Title	Qty.	Total
The Streets and San Man's Guide	_____ @ $12.95 =	_____
Chicago Haunts	_____ @ $15.00 =	_____
More Chicago Haunts	_____ @ $15.00 =	_____
Graveyards of Chicago	_____ @ $15.00 =	_____
The Firefigher's Best Friend	_____ @ $19.95 =	_____
A Cook's Guide to Chicago	_____ @ $15.00 =	_____
Creepy Chicago	_____ @ $ 8.00 =	_____
Great Chicago Fires	_____ @ $19.95 =	_____
Chicago's Midway Airport	_____ @ $19.95 =	_____
Hollywood on Lake Michigan	_____ @ $15.00 =	_____
_____	_____ @ $_____ =	_____

Subtotal:_____
Less Discount: _____
New Subtotal: _____
8.75% Sales Tax for Illinois Residents:_____
Shipping: _____
TOTAL: _____

Please enclose check, money order, or credit card information.

Name _____

Address _____

City _____ State _____ Zip _____

Visa/MC/AmEx/Disc.# _____ Exp. _____

Signature _____

PURCHASE MULTIPLE COPIES AND SAVE!	**LOW SHIPPING FEES**
2 books — 10% discount	• $2.50 for the first book
3–4 books — 20% discount	• $.50 for each additional book
5–9 books — 25% discount	• Maximum charge: $8.00
10+ books — 40% discount	

LAKE CLAREMONT PRESS

4650 N. Rockwell St.
Chicago, IL 60625
773/583-7800 • 773/583-7877 (fax)
lcp@lakeclaremont.com
www.lakeclaremont.com

ABOUT THE
AUTHOR

Dennis Foley, a life-long Chicagoan, wrote *The Streets and San Man's Guide to Chicago Eats* during his six-year tenure as an electrician in the City of Chicago's Department of Streets and Sanitation. He received his MFA in Creative Writing from Columbia College—Chicago, and his work has appeared in *Poetry Motel*, *Hair Trigger 23* and *24*, *Block's Magazine*, *The Use of Personal Narratives in the Helping Profession*, *Gravity*, *Bluelit.com*, and a number of other publications. Now working primarily as a freelance writer, Dennis is happily married to Susan, and they have three boys, Matt–15, Pat–12, and Mike–4. Dennis also coaches basketball at his alma mater, St. Laurence High School. He firmly believes that lunch is a very important part of the day.